Fostering Brand Community Through Social Media

Fostering Brand Community Through Social Media

William F. Humphrey, Jr., Debra A. Laverie, and Shannon B. Rinaldo

BUSINESS EXPERT PRESS

Fostering Brand Community Through Social Media

Copyright © Business Expert Press, LLC, 2016.

First published in 2016 by
Business Expert Press, LLC
222 East 46th Street, New York, NY 10017
www.businessexpertpress.com

ISBN-13: 978-1-60649-940-5 (paperback)
ISBN-13: 978-1-60649-941-2 (e-book)

Business Expert Press Digital and Social Media Marketing and Advertising Collection

Collection ISSN: 2333-8822 (print)
Collection ISSN: 2333-8830 (electronic)

Cover and interior design by Exeter Premedia Services Private Ltd., Chennai, India

First edition: 2016

10 9 8 7 6 5 4 3 2 1

Printed in the United States of America.

Abstract

This book focuses on building and maintaining brand community in the emerging, dynamic space of social media. A theoretical model encompassing brand characteristics, relational factors, and characteristics of the brand user community is used as a structure to explain the various aspects of online brand communities. Furthermore, the authors discuss how online brand communities differ from and can be used to complement traditional, face-to-face brand communities. Brand managers, social media managers, and other members of the brand team will find this book useful for strategic decision-making in both building and maintaining brand communities. In addition, this book will serve as a practical guide for working professionals enrolled in executive education degree programs as these programs continue to be developed in universities throughout the world.

Keywords

Branding, brand community, customer service, Facebook, Foursquare, Instagram, Pinterest, Snapchat, social media, Twitter

Contents

Acknowledgments

Special thanks to our official editor Vicki Crittendon and our personal editor Diane Krumwiede.

CHAPTER 1

The Online Brand Community

Social media is a powerful tool in the Integrated Marketing Communications mix. Companies cultivate fans on Facebook, respond to tweets on Twitter, and encourage consumers to post their brand interactions on Pinterest. Managing the social media platform is a delicate balance for many companies, especially since consumers control much of the content. So how can companies manage their online relationships with customers in a way that can lead to brand loyalty? We present a conceptual model to detail factors managers should consider in using social media to build brand community. We discuss the benefits of a strong brand community and offer examples of how brands are effectively building community through social media. The following discussion is based on theory, academic research, and practice.

A brand community is a specialized community where the "primary base of identification is a brand or brand consumption activity."[1] These communities are growing as brand managers have increasingly focused on consumers' relationships with brands.[2] Brand community is a prominent form of consumer–brand relationship[3] where brand users with similar interests and experiences come together in a social group.[4] The community is a focused community that is not geographically bound; it is grounded in social relationships among users of a particular brand. One thing that sets brand communities apart from other social clubs is the brand. The community is most often formed around a publicly consumed brand, rather than a product that is consumed in private.

Brand communities are built on a sense of emotional involvement with the brand and the group. These communities engage in actions that often are related to common goals. For instance, there are many brand communities focused on the Jeep brand. These consumers gather, interact, and together pursue activities to see what extremes they can pit their Jeeps through (trail riding, rock climbing, and water passings). They provide support and recommendations, and engage in sharing brand experiences. Brand communities form their own norms and rituals. Interaction in a community increases feelings of integration into the Jeep brand community and positive feelings about the product category and the brand. Participants derive social and hedonic value from participation and often participate in product alterations and design.

Companies encourage brand admirers and strengthen consumer relationships with one another as well as the brand to create brand communities. The now-defunct automobile brand Saturn was the first automobile company to create a community. The company devoted considerable resources (e.g., money, people, time, and events) to build the brand community. Saturn owners were invited annually to the company's Springhill, Tennessee (USA) plant, where the Saturn drivers enjoyed company-sponsored activities, gathered with other drivers, and met the people who made their cars. The goal of these gatherings was to strengthen the "Saturn Family" as well as the Saturn brand. The thought was that the more connected drivers felt to one another and the brand, the more likely they were to stay loyal when purchasing their next vehicle. On the other hand, brand communities can emerge organically. Organic brand communities are analogous to fan clubs where individuals with mutual admiration for an entity come together to share information, knowledge, experience, and identity without explicit sanctioning from the company managing the brand.[5]

Brand communities may also get their beginnings as consumer-created, but later gain support from the company. The first Corvette-related club was started in 1956, three years after the first cars rolled off the assembly line. According to the website for the Corvette Club of America, the goals of the club included promoting Corvette ownership, operation, and knowledge. Although many consumer-maintained Corvette brand communities still exist, the Corvette plant in Bowling Green, Kentucky (USA) has hosted a "Homecoming" annually since 1980 and actively supports the National Council of Corvette Clubs, an organization of more than 275 smaller clubs with the motto "We joined for the car, we stay for the people." These brand communities create a unique form of brand equity.

Brand Communities and Social Media

Brand managers have long understood that relational and experiential aspects of consumption are important for building relationships with consumers.[6] Historically, companies looking to foster brand loyalty focused on using advertising, direct mail, and other traditional media effectively. Companies who supported brand communities typically did so through the president of a club, who in turn disseminated brand information to members. As the modern consumer moved online, the historical tenets of brand community have evolved. The rapid and widespread adoption of social media and digital marketing now provides brand stewards with a rich and interactive environment in which to build, maintain, and monitor communities. Social media and digital applications offer a rich environment where consumers can start and maintain their own brand communities, engage with brands and other members, and companies can interact with members of the community directly. Online interactions are instant, and this provides an environment where communities are able to grow quickly, sometimes literally overnight. Marketers today have a distinctive advantage to create value in brand communities using social media by leveraging two-way communications that didn't previously exist.

Traditional brand community members were restricted by location. Connected consumers in a community, brand or otherwise, do not face these same geographic restrictions as consumers from around the world can interact in these digital forums. As brands continue to play an increasingly important role in consumers' purchasing decisions, brand communities help companies identify the perceived social image of consumers.[7] Members of a community interact (in-person or online) and can create a sense of "we-ness" or felt connection to the brand, the company, and the community.[8] As connected consumers interact, a reference group emerges, and community members connect in a way that is relevant to one another. The interactions lead connected consumers to identify with one another and with the brand, and form a community.

Social media and digital connectivity help consumers and brands communicate more efficiently with technology to facilitate the sharing of information through online social connections.[9] Online communities, such as those facilitated via social media sites, provide the perfect platform to build relationships through customer interactions.[10] Examining social media in relation to brand communities seems a logical progression, as word of mouth via social media is acknowledged as being as influential, if not more influential, than conventional word-of-mouth communication.[11] Strong emphasis in the marketplace on the importance of social media leads us to examine its role in building and maintaining brand communities.

Today consumers are informed, time-compressed, and difficult to impress. Contemporary consumers are more likely to be influenced by someone in their social network than a celebrity endorser.[12] Connected consumers seek authentic social interactions with other consumers about the brands that matter to them.[13] Through this peer-to-peer interaction via online brand communities, marketers gain unique glimpses into the important roles brands play in the lives of consumers. In a community, connected consumers interact with both the firm and other consumers within the community.

The most heavily used form of social media is Facebook.[14] Facebook lists its active user base at over a billion users of whom over half log on daily. The average user has 130 friends, and participants collectively spend over 700 billion minutes per month on Facebook.[15] Facebook's popularity and transcendence makes it a crucial platform for developing brand communities.[16] While Facebook is the exemplar social network, brand managers must consider the other key channels such as Twitter and Pinterest to engage the connected consumer. One channel does not fit all consumer needs. Twitter is a microblog site that features an ongoing stream of 140 character updates.[17] Consumers increasingly use Twitter to interact with brands and other consumers regarding brands. There are over 500 million active users of Twitter. A study conducted by Millward Brown Digital in 2013 found that over 50 percent of users expect an answer back from a brand on Twitter within an hour of their post. This number rises to over 70 percent if the post is a complaint. The study found that a brand's response time to a tweet could significantly impact the brands' reputation.

Another important platform is Pinterest, a social network where users curate images from web links. Pinterest has been credited with driving more referral traffic than multiple other networks combined.[18] There are a number of reasons why brands use Pinterest: brand awareness, brand equity, and ultimately customer retention. Pinterest offers a visually, aesthetically pleasing user experience where consumers curate boards of favorite brands. However, Pinterest is more focused on images of objects rather than relationships. While these trends of consumer engagement on various social media sites show promise for brands, brand managers must competently adapt and specialize their messages on other social media sites to address considerations such as medium-specific message requirements and the asynchronous nature of these communications.[19] Please see Table 1.1 for a glossary of social media sites, both current and retired.

Building Blocks of an Online Brand Community

It is well recognized that developing ongoing relationships with customers can lead to brand loyalty.[20] Brand managers are building successful online brand communities using social media and digital applications. Our model outlines specific factors for consideration as firms move toward building community online: brand characteristics, relational characteristics, and community characteristics (Figure 1.1). In order for brand communities to flourish, brands first need to be competent, have a strong reputation, and be perceived as representing high quality.[21] These brand characteristics lead to high identity salience and brand identification for the consumer. Relational characteristics refer to how well consumers identify with the brand, their brand experiences, the amount and nature of their social media exposure, and how relevant both the reference group and the marketing messages are to the consumers. The relevance of the reference group and the relevance of the message will influence identification with others in the community and identity importance, which in turn build brand community. Relevant community characteristics are how well individuals identify with others in the group and the salience

Table 1.1 Glossary of social media sites

Site	Type	Description	Status
Facebook	Community	Page and newsfeed-based social media site with dedicated brand pages.	Active
Twitter	Stream	140-character stream of social media updates with the abilty to reply, private message, share links, and reshare content from others.	Active
Instagram	Image	Primarily mobile network with photos shared. Filters and editing tools available. Owned by Facebook.	Active
Snapchat	Image or Video	Started as a six-second video or image site with finger-written captions to select users. Now includes updates that can be longer and open to all participants (used by brands). Viewed Snapchats are supposed to be erased by the site permanently.	Active
MySpace	Community	Original community site that featured participant pages and friends. Relaunched as a music-focused site, but considered a dying site.	Dying
LinkedIn	Community	Online resume site that allows participants to connect with professional contacts. Used heavily by recruiters with job posting functionality.	Active
Vine	Video	Six-second video vignettes shared to followers. Brands sponsor popular Vine personalities to promote products. Owned by Twitter.	Active
Google+	Community	Community site that leverages Gmail and Google sign-in. Never took off and is being dismantled. Google Places pages migrated to this platform.	Dying
Secret	Anonymous	Participants anonymously choose image and add text to share secrets.	Dead
YikYak	Anonymous	Student-focused anonymous platform that can include images.	Active
Yeti	Anonymous	Snapchat-like network that shows short videos or images with text, but only within certain geographic boundaries.	Active

Slack	Community	Project-based business community that allows asynchronous collaboration of a team. Includes blog posts, attachments, and private messaging.	Active
Yammer	Community	Microsoft's team collaboration tool designed for enterprise cross-functional teams. Integrates into Office 365.	Active
Yelp	Review	Business review site that allows consumers to review businesses and upload photos. Businesses can claim pages, upload details on the business, and respond to reviews.	Active
TripAdvisor	Review	Travel centric review website that curates top hotels by city and awards specific properties with accolades they can use in marketing. Businesses can claim pages, upload details on the business, and respond to reviews.	Active
Foursquare	Review	Originally launched as a gamified location check-in service. Now serves as a more succinct, Twitter-length review site. Relies on users to provide location information and tips. Businesses can claim pages, upload details on the business, and respond to reviews. Gamified experience now on Swarm. Serves as source of location information for other social sites, such as Twitter.	Active
Swarm	Location	Users check-in to locations to share where they're at and the experiences they're enjoying. Top visitors are deemed mayor, and specific actions unlock gamified badges.	Active
Gowalla	Location	Users check-in to locations to share where they're at and the experiences they're enjoying. Virtual scavenger hunt allows users to collect items. Sold to Facebook and discontinued.	Dead
Loopt	Location	Users check-in to locations to share where they're at and the experiences they're enjoying.	Dead
Grindr	Dating or Location	Participants see a grid of others nearby sorted by distance. Photo share capabilities augment the main profile picture. Targeted to gay men.	Active
Scruff	Dating or Location	Participants see a grid of others nearby sorted by distance. Photo share capabilities augment the main profile picture. Targeted to hairy or scruffy gay men.	Active

(Continued)

Table 1.1 Glossary of social media sites **(Continued)**

Site	Type	Description	Status
Tinder	Dating or Location	Participants see a grid of others nearby sorted by distance. Users swipe to hide or indicate a match with others. Targeted to heterosexuals.	Active
Ping	Music	Apple's short-lived iTunes-based music social network.	Dead
Diaspora	Community	Facebook-like community targeted to participants seeking privacy and lack of marketing messages.	Dead
Path	Image	Image-sharing social network that limited participants to a certain number of quality connections.	Dying
Google Buzz	Microblog	Syndicated content from a participant's other social media profiles. Criticized for privacy issues.	Dead

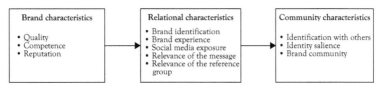

Figure 1.1 Building online brand community requires brand, relational, and community characteristics

of the brand-based identity. We believe that when nurtured, these factors will lead to robust brand communities.

Chapter 2 further discusses how brand quality, competence, and reputation are the primary building blocks for brand communities. Chapter 3 focuses on what we refer to as "relational characteristics," the consumers' experiences and identification with the brand, the amount and nature of online exposure, and how relevant the message content and the reference group are to consumers. Chapter 4 examines how the elements of Chapters 2 and 3 lead to community characteristics, namely identifying with others and identity salience, to result in a more successful brand community. Chapter 5 posits that online brand community building provides advantages over traditional brand community strategy. In this chapter, several examples of successful online approaches are highlighted. Chapter 6 explores differences between brand fans versus consumers, the power of customer service, and dealing with complaints on social media and digital platforms. Chapter 7 ties together the previous chapters and develops a cohesive summary of how to foster brand community through social media. Furthermore, we consider what the future will bring for social media and brand communities.

CHAPTER 2

Brand Characteristics

How to Communicate Quality, Competence, and Reputation via Social Media

Firm size and market share do not appear to be factors in building strong communities, as both small and large companies have built successful communities of brand-loyal consumers. Many of these companies, particularly those with limited resources, have done so via social media. The accessibility of digital media lowers the barriers to entry and places small brands on a level playing field with larger brands for cultivating online communities of fans. Brands likely to successfully form and foster brand community must first exhibit strong performance in the key brand factors of: quality, competence, and reputation. For a consumer to simply hit the "Like" button on Facebook or follow a brand on Twitter is a low-commitment action, but a higher level relationship is possible when a consumer engages with a high quality, competent, and reputable brand. While Facebook has made the "Like" function ubiquitous as the method for endorsing content or following company's content, the brand must achieve these key brand factors before consumers actually want to engage online. Simply clicking "Like" on a page does not guarantee that consumers identify with the brand or engage with the brand community.

With over one billion participants liking and commenting an average 3.2 billion times per day on Facebook, brands have a strong motivation to develop and communicate key brand factors to potential online brand fans.[1] In the following discussion, we focus on brand interactions where the brand gives consumers tangible reasons to care about the brand's quality, competence, and reputation. In turn, consumers engage with the brand and other fans online in an involved manner.

Quality

If consumers are interested in joining a brand community and associating themselves with the brand in online communities via social networks like Twitter and Facebook, brands must first entice consumers with a quality product and consumption experience. Logically, a brand must first have a quality product or service to warrant engaging consumers in social media. Quality is a necessary first step in luring consumers to identify with a brand.

Quality is defined as a consumer's judgments about excellence.[2] In marketing, quality is measured by the difference between consumer's expectations and the performance of the product.[3] Therefore, the mere existence of a social media profile can signal certain minimum standards about brand quality in the mind of the consumer. A large following and frequent interaction on a digital profile further increases quality perception. Applications where consumers access brand information and interact with products and services further signal quality.

Direct messages on brand quality may also be disseminated by the brand. For example, each month, the President and CEO of Volvo selects a story to share as part of the "Volvo Saved My Life" campaign (Figure 2.1). This campaign uses social channels to reinforce the core brand value of safety through quality.[4] Sourced through nonsocial media channels, these authentic stories of how a Volvo automobile saved the lives of one or more customers regularly reinforces key advertising and features messages that Volvos are the safest on the road. By making this feature recurring, brand fans are reminded that they have made the best decision to champion this brand. In turn, the fan network sees the interaction and endorsement of the brand via Facebook likes, shares, and comments.

As brand fans who "like" the Volvo Cars U.S. Facebook page or "like" the update, share the update with their friends or leave a comment, the fans' networks view these actions as endorsements and the message of brand quality is shared. Consumers interact with one another by replying to fan comments and contributing to the Volvo-originated content. As brand fans endorse the message of quality and safety in Volvo's case, the brand's message is corroborated and perpetuated.

Figure 2.1 Volvo saved my life

Fan comments can also serve as de facto testimonials via social media. On Facebook, the comments can be shared or quoted to the fan base of the brand's page; on Twitter, the brands may reply with a verbatim quote of the message or retweet to the brand's followers. For domestic airline Virgin America, a sampling of tweets shows positive commentary from both celebrities and everyday consumer fliers.[5] Many of these tweets reflect consumer perceptions of quality (Figure 2.2).

Consumer-originated messages (like the ones in the figure) can be spread on Twitter by brands in two primary ways: (1) the brand can retweet comments to increase exposure or (2) followers of the brand fans originating the comment can retweet and share with their followers. In both cases, the message of quality is disseminated to a wider audience through electronic word of mouth.

Digital applications also communicate quality and encourage consumer–brand interaction. For example, the Mary Kay Makeover mobile application allows fans to virtually experiment with Mary Kay products. Mobile users can use an existing photo or their own uploaded photo and apply Mary Kay products to the photo. In addition, users

Figure 2.2 *Virgin America consumer communications of quality via endorsements*

Figure 2.3 *Screenshots from Mary Kay's mobile application*

can compare different makeup configurations, save makeup configurations, share their creations via social media or e-mail, offer feedback to Mary Kay about the company's products, application, or both, and even purchase the products directly from the application (Figure 2.3). These types of applications communicate quality for brands. In a similar sense, this application communicates the competence of the Mary Kay brand. Competence is discussed in the next section.

Competence

Like quality, competence is necessary for a brand to merit engagement with fans on social media and the two often go together, as demonstrated in the Mary Kay Mobile App example. A brand possesses competence when it has strong capabilities to carry out intentions and to engage in successful business practices.[6] Consistent competence in performance is often an antecedent to trust, as competence is associated with reduced uncertainty and ambiguity.[7] Furthermore, perceived competence will lead to greater identification with the brands among consumers.[8] For instance, if a consumer perceives competence compared to other brands, this competence increases the extent to which consumers identify with the brand. As consumers discover the salient characteristics that distinguish a brand as more competent than other brands, it enhances the attractiveness of the brand to consumers. Research has shown that the competence of the company is associated with strong brand identification.[9]

Experiential and intangible products benefit most from online commentary because consumers are likely to share their experiences and opinions on social media sites. Digital platforms provide consumers the opportunity to judge and comment on brand competence for others to witness.[10] One indicator of competence is service delivery. Positive experiences of service delivery may not receive nearly as much recognition and word of mouth as does negative customer interactions. Traditionally, unhappy consumers have told far more people of their experience than have happy consumers. However, when consumers can communicate directly with brands, many of them take the time to recognize when a brand has performed competently. Some brands, like American Express, have dedicated customer service channels in social media, such as the @askamex Twitter account (Figure 2.4). When a customer has had successful problem resolution through social channels, they will often tweet praise, such as this exchange between American Express and a card member on Twitter.[11]

Figure 2.4 Ask Amex responds to a consumer tweet

A competent response from the company allows the brand to reinforce the positive relationship with the consumer in question and share the positive feedback with the brand's other fans and followers. Competence in handling customers, when executed flawlessly on social media, increases customer satisfaction. Situations in which the brand goes above and beyond to resolve a customer issue online can result in additional word of mouth praising the brand. This type of positive feedback builds goodwill beyond what can be fostered through advertising programs.

In business-to-business interactions, key updates via social media allow the firm to communicate product or policy updates to agents or resellers. This takes form as corporate business-to-business social media accounts or a corporate executive page. Royal Caribbean International highlights its competence in business-to-business relationships via its Senior Vice President of Sales and Trade Support and Services, Vicki Freed.[12] The executive communication through Facebook signals competence through ongoing communications on timely updates, like product enhancements, training webinars, and advertising support materials. Competence is also demonstrated via the two-way dialogue with travel agents, who are their primary business-to-business clients. The sales staff gets immediate and unfiltered feedback through social media comments to Freed's page, and problems can be quickly addressed and resolved. Additionally, the brand executive's social media serves as an additional executive voice in times of brand crisis as a personal way to supplement traditional corporate communications (Figure 2.5).

Engagement and proactive communication through social channels signal competence, and perceived competence justifies future brand interaction through social media online. More companies are demonstrating that digital media can be used in a business-to-business context as effectively as in the business-to-consumer context.

Reputation

The third critical brand-related factor for consideration for building brand community online is brand reputation. Reputation has been defined as "a consumer's overall evaluation of a [brand] based on his or her reactions to the [brand's] goods, services, communication activities, interactions."[13]

Figure 2.5 Royal Caribbean engages in executive communication via Facebook

Because communication activities and interactions occur online, digital media is a crucial platform for building and maintaining reputation. Furthermore, a solid reputation is the stepping-stone to building loyal consumers and creating brand identity in the minds of consumers.[14] Therefore, consumer interactions with and consumption of the brand online lead to trust and identity, two factors crucial for building brand community.[15] Although brand quality and competence contribute to a brand's reputation, interaction between the brand and consumers contributes significantly to how brand fans perceive a brand's overall reputation. Consumers influence a brand's reputation with assessments and evaluations of a brand's product or service delivery, and social media facilitates this assessment seamlessly. By sharing brand experiences with their network through social media, consumers contribute both positively and negatively to a brand's reputation.

Uber is a transportation networking company and mobile application used to connect riders with vehicles for hire or others interested in ridesharing. This service may be used as a one-time taxi alternative or as a regular carpooling option. Uber has built a reputation on high levels of service and a clean, safe ride. This reputation has been strengthened with the online testimonies of users. Uber rides can only be booked via the mobile app, which means the firm's customers are digitally savvy. By exceeding customer expectations for this connected consumer base, Uber enjoys regular feedback through social media channels when expectations are exceeded.[16] Unsolicited positive feedback serves to attract new users and, thus, new fans of the service. In addition, having high profile clients ensures that Uber's reputation as a safe, clean driver alternative spreads beyond early adopters. These influential consumers have cultivated large audiences that trust their product suggestions and recommendations. As influential consumers share their brand experiences online, reputation is built (or damaged) based on the perception of the brand.

Although social media networks Facebook and Twitter offer excellent examples of how brands influence consumer perceptions of quality, competence, and reputation for building brand community, there are many other digital platforms where these activities take place. User review sites like TripAdvisor and Yelp are very influential in signaling quality, competence, and reputation, and mobile location social networks like Foursquare influence consumers by suggesting popular locations and businesses a participant might like based on locations that their social network has frequented. If the brand's website features ratings and reviews, this also provides an excellent forum for consumers to share their brand experiences and influence prospective customers. This forum (along with Yelp and TripAdvisor) also allows brand managers to engage and reply to both the good and the bad. The exchange in Figure 2.6 occurred between a past guest and the Sheraton Gunter Hotel in San Antonio, Texas. The guest posted several positive comments about her stay related to her room, the location, and the service in the bar.[17] In turn, the hotel social media team responded with a personal message. If the goal of relationship marketing is to extend positive relationships indefinitely, then responding to the positive feedback is highly encouraged whether online or otherwise.[18]

While no brand will have perfect service delivery 100 percent of the time, responding to consumers on social media channels and on brand-sponsored review forums allows for an authentic exchange between brand and consumer. If a brand has a social media presence, consumers expect two-way dialogues, response, or both, when a concern is raised. As early as 2008, consumer sentiment held that 93 percent of consumers expected a brand to be on social media and 85 percent expected a response from brands in social media.[19] While brand managers hope that

Figure 2.6 Responding to positive feedback builds reputation

consumers will complain about a negative experience to them first, it has become incredibly easy for consumers to complain to friends and strangers instantly. Thus it becomes critical that brands allocate resources to monitor online reputation and respond to both the good and the bad. Whereas customer service once was a one-to-one exchange that was private between the customer and brand, all consumers now have the means to see social media complaints and resolution (if brands respond appropriately).

Social media cannot create the quality, competence, or reputation of a brand, but it can powerfully signal each of these factors to consumers if messaged strategically in social channels. Digital media also can effectively uncover incompetence, poor quality, and perpetuate a bad reputation through consumer conversation and electronic word of mouth. In order to persuasively signal the three key brand factors in a positive direction, the social media approach of a brand must be savvy and competent since digitally engaged consumers see through lame or incompetent social media campaigns and interactions. Simply retweeting or sharing praise does not create a compelling story to convince a skeptical and media-saturated consumer of the positives of a brand. Once these three brand characteristics are present, brands should focus on relational characteristics (discussed in subsequent chapters) before embarking on the necessary community characteristics for building an effective brand community.

Based on this initial discussion of brand factors, the following observations are some best practices social media and brand managers can glean for past successes.

Key Takeaways

- Share content that reinforces the key brand factors of quality, competence, and reputation.
- Allow the fans of the brand to do the talking—leverage consumer testimonials, whether sourced online via social media or offline via e-mail, telephone, or other traditional servicing channels.
- Use ratings and reviews on the brand website to help consumers make informed choices; a transparent, authentic forum reflects well on the brand.
- Solicit content such as tips, suggestions from the products or services of a brand, or full reviews of a brand experience.
- Social media can work in business-to-business contexts; regular updates and interaction with the trade channels can serve as an authentic way to show a long-term business commitment.
- Reply to both the good and the bad in user-generated content; prospects considering the brand will intuit that they will be treated similarly to those receiving replies in social and in review forums.
- Don't expect social media to be a silver bullet; the firm must have quality, competence, and a good reputation to warrant positive social feedback.
- Fostering the three key brand factors leads to consumer identification with a brand; once a consumer identifies with a brand, social media interactions and exposure are likely to occur (Chapter 3).

CHAPTER 3

Relational Characteristics in Social Media

Brand Experiences, Exposure, Relevance of the Message, and Relevance of the Group

Relational characteristics serve as mediators between brand characteristics and community characteristics. The first step is creating a brand that is well promoted and perceived as high quality, competent, and reputable online. Next, brand managers should spend time enriching brand experiences, through social media exposure and relevant messages. This chapter defines each of these relational factors and discusses how they are interrelated, affect consumers, and are influenced by the brand manager online.

Brand Experiences

First and foremost, consumers must have experience with the brand initially before forming a desire to interact with a brand online.[1] The binding factor in relationships between people and brands is emotion. Consumers connect with a brand if the feel affect associated with the brand. When consumers identify with a brand, they desire experiences with the brand and with other users of that brand. This is where social media becomes an ideal forum for building this interaction, which ultimately leads to brand community. Consumer identities can be tied with brands, in that brands contribute to an individual's sense of self (and the identity they portray in various situations). Brand identification discussed in the next section leads one to take on the emotional process of developing identity through consumption experiences.[2] In turn, these experiences drive consumers to seek relevant online reference groups and the brand becomes even more salient to the consumer, leading down the path of a stronger and more durable bond between consumer and brand.[3] The following sections identify how brands foster these experiences and incrementally strengthen relationships with consumers.

Types of Social Media Exposure

Exposure can occur in forms varying from the standard status update on Facebook to a six-second video vignette on the social network Vine. The original goal of social media was for consumers to connect and communicate with friends and family. Social media includes advertising that is akin to traditional online advertising, brand interactions with consumers, and consumer-to-consumer endorsement of brands. There are key types of social media exposure brands can undertake in the hopes of fostering positive brand-to-consumer, consumer-to-brand, and consumer-to-consumer interactions on various social channels. These different types include: content sharing, implied endorsement, customer service interactions, video vignettes, location updates, and paid advertising. For the greatest generalizability of these concepts, the exposure types are grouped by type of communication, not by the specific social network.

Content Sharing

The most common exposure in social media is content shared by a brand on social media. With over 1.4 billion active users, Facebook currently has the greatest reach of any social media network. Content shared by brands on Facebook can include status updates, images, videos, and links to content on other social networks. Content with images or video can gain great traction, and the image below serves as an example. Samsung Mobile USA posted an image (Figure 3.1) demonstrating how to use its Galaxy Gear smart watch with the simple caption of "Behold the many faces of Galaxy Gear."[4]

Figure 3.1 Galaxy Gear shares images of its smart watch

Figure 3.2 Coca-Cola responds to Mashable on Twitter

Even a simple execution such as this resulted in over 29,000 likes and over 1,600 shares. While Samsung Mobile USA has over 26 million fans on Facebook,[5] the sharing of this post had extensive reach. This strategy is also prevalent on Twitter. Recent updates have allowed content such as images and videos to play in the browser or app window for more effective content. For example, Coca-Cola responded to new media blog Mashable about a recent article and included a visual image branded Coca-Cola, as shown in Figure 3.2.[6]

In addition, visual images are shared regularly via Instagram and Pinterest, and this content can be easily reshared to a network member's audience. Icons for each of the major social networks typically appear below a participant's post, and this mechanism is the ubiquitous method for syndicating content to a person's other social networks. In 2015, Pinterest announced the launch of functionality to allow participants to buy products directly from the site, with 2 million products available at launch.[7] This initiative allows consumers to easily buy products they like through consumer recommendation, and it augments Pinterest's advertising revenue strategy.

Implied Endorsement

For each person who shares, likes, or comments on content shared by a brand, each member of his or her network has an opportunity to see this brand interaction through the Facebook Newsfeed. Additionally, in the right pane of Facebook, a live feed of friend activity (such as page likes, page interaction, music consumed, etc.) scrolls constantly, increasing the chance that a person's network will see interactions with a brand page's content. Potential reach of specific content is calculated using: (1) the number of social media users who like the page and (2) the total number of friends in network by users interacting with that content. Actual reach includes the actual number of brand fans who saw the content and the total number of friends of brand fans who saw their brand interaction through the newsfeed or other means. In Figure 3.3, the reach number of interactions includes likes, comments, and shares (respectively) on Facebook, but does not include the incidental exposure that comes from members of each of those participants' networks.

A market maven is a thought leader related to product categories and marketplaces who shares product purchase and use advice.[8] If a Facebook user is considered to be influential (i.e., a market maven), that user is likely to influence his or her network so that the network develops a more positive evaluation of the brand. Therefore, content shared can have a snowball effect, much like the sharing from the Galaxy Gear image. Brands want influential consumers to like and share the brand's content so that they gain exposure to friends of their brand fans. Therefore, finding the best content and proper execution is critical. Creating compelling content that mavens want to share helps diffuse the brand message to a wider audience.

👍 29,320   💬 692   🔗 1,681

Figure 3.3 Social media platforms communicate message reach

Customer Service Interactions

Customer service exchanges between customers and service providers are a key type of social media interaction. As mentioned in the discussion on competence, consumers expect that brands will respond in social media channels. This is particularly true for customer service exchanges. Social media has a wide reach, including the consumer engaging with the brand, other consumers who access the brand's social media page, and those customers' networks. Effective, prompt, and positive customer service handling is critical in today's world with social media exposure. Prior to the widespread adoption of social media, customer complaining was largely a private affair. The consumer would interact with the company via the call center, e-mail, website form, or slow mail. The complaining consumer might share complaints with others through traditional word-of-mouth communication; however, service interaction was typically between the consumer and the brand. Social media has shifted power from the firm to the consumer. When a consumer complains via social media by tweeting about a problem or posting dissatisfaction on a brand's Facebook wall, the customer service interaction becomes a public exchange. Others' opinions may be influenced by incidental exposure to social media interactions between the brand and another consumer. This voyeurism has the potential to change both opinions and preferences for these secondary consumers. Brands can benefit from the positive word of mouth on social media. Therefore, brands are wise to invest in ways to service social media complainers.

When brands interact with consumers and proactively try to resolve problems for the consumer, they signal to other social media users that all complaints will be handled in the same manner. Conversely, ignoring a social media complaint signals that the company would extend that same apathy to other consumers. In many cases, brands attempt to push the discussion off the social channel into another servicing method. In Figure 3.4, American Express's @AskAmex Twitter account "follows" the customer so the communication can be conducted via private direct message. The representative invites the consumer to chat via AmericanExpress.com, which requires the consumer to log in and authenticate himself or herself. Pulling the consumer into the

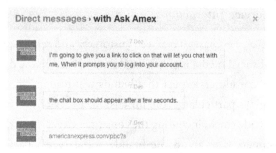

Figure 3.4 Ask Amex communicates with consumers via direct message (DM)

authenticated signed-in site allows the service agent to see account information, customer spending, and history with the brand.

This method for handling customer problems makes intuitive sense. The brand expresses concern and a desire to resolve the issue in the open channel, and then the conversation is taken offline. Another effective technique for pushing the discussion offline is to provide a contact for the service team handling social media, as opposed to the general customer service group. The public communication is that the social media team will handle the issue if the customer e-mails them. This signals to the consumer that the team he or she tweeted or posted to will investigate or handle the issue. Avis uses this approach with a dedicated e-mail to the service members of the social media team when a consumer complains via social media.[9]

A less effective method is to ask consumers to call the brand's call center. If a consumer has previously not received resolution through other channels, then prompting him or her to use a previously unsuccessful channel will alienate the consumer. Often, if a consumer is tweeting the brand, he or she is in this exact scenario, having already attempted other channels without satisfactory resolution. Even a fast response can make the situation worse, particularly when the consumer is asked to call in.

Video Vignettes

Gaining rapid adoption among social media users, Twitter's owned Vine tool gained 12 million users in the first four months.[10] Videos shot from mobile devices, either continuously or in stop motion, are shared on the Vine network and syndicated by users onto other networks such as Twitter and Facebook. Brands have found success in recruiting popular video contributors to create content that is likely to be shared and liked, such as the Just Dance video game promotion in Figure 3.5.[11] In a mere six seconds, creative social media participants can create content that costs a fraction of the cost of traditional media and can gain significant sharing. Popular Vine contributors have earned up to $10,000 for their six-second videos and now have access to a talent agency that will broker out the Vine contributors' services.[12] Vine has quickly become an important element in social media.[13]

To compete with Twitter's Vine offering, Facebook launched a similar feature on its visual network Instagram in 2013. The primary difference between Vine and the Instagram version is the length of the videos. In Instagram, videos may be up to 15 seconds.[14] While these networks currently have limited reach, the ubiquitous share to Facebook and Twitter helps brands extend their reach (and any investment in content creation they make). Additionally, brands are exploring how to reach

Figure 3.5 Consumer-created video content

younger, mobile consumers via Snapchat, a social network that allows participants to share short videos or images that are finite in duration (or disappear after viewing). Brands exploring this platform include CNN, ESPN, People, Buzzfeed, and iHeartRadio. This service lists 60 percent of mobile users between 13 and 34 years of age as being Snapchat users, and over 4 billion video views consumed daily.[15]

Location Updates

As recent as a decade ago, marketing scholars declared that the "place" component of the four Ps marketing mix was dead. These critics proclaimed that the global reach of the Internet made location irrelevant to marketing.[16] With widespread adoption of mobile technology and deep integration of global positioning satellite functionality, location has regained significance.[17] Today, status updates on most social media platforms can be tagged with locations, including Facebook statuses and tweets. Two closely related location-based social networks, Swarm and Foursquare, have integrated social updates with a person's physical location. While at a store or restaurant location, participants can share their location with both users on both sites and their wider network (via Facebook, Twitter, or both). This content can be in the form of a "check-in," which is essentially a status update showing where the person is located. Consumers can also share tips with their networks concerning what to do, what to buy, or what to expect so that other users may use the experience in their information search. Location-based social media platforms use crowdsourced information databases created by its users. Users create and update the locations on the social media platform. Rather than keep the database as a proprietary asset, Foursquare licenses its database to other apps, including Vine and Foodspotting. This allows the users to add to the content and share their experience with their network. Location sharing is available on mobile as well as on web-based updates made on a desktop or notebook computer. As of 2014, Swarm serves as the location check-in feature, and Foursquare serves as a source of location reviews, tips, and images. Users of either app are able to navigate seamlessly from one app to the other from check-in to consumption of reviews.

As with implied endorsement, location updates can signal user's networks as to feelings toward a store or restaurant. Furthermore, this signal can influence the network, particularly when the user is influential within that network. If the participant is seen as influential in a product category, his or her tips or insights may be more powerful at influencing the network (as with the traditional market maven concept). Business owners can "claim" their Swarm page. This allows proprietors insight into the frequency of visitors, the most frequent visitor, and how visitors might be influencing others. Managers can access Foursquare's business "dashboard," where they can learn participants' social media account information. Having the participants' social media account information allows the business to recognize loyal customers with rewards and welcome first time visitors with specials and promotions. As brands seek to promote community formation, this type of two-way communication becomes essential. As network participants contribute tips and visual content, they further contribute to the online and mobile reputation discussed in Chapter 1.

Paid Advertising and Sponsored Content

Social media platforms have continuously sought ways to capitalize on the active user base, and a key element of this monetization has been advertising. On Facebook, primary forms of paid advertising include display ads (shown on the right side of the computer interface platform) and sponsored content or suggested pages. Display ads can be easily created using the online tools for page administrators. Ads may display on Facebook pages (to generate a like by nonfans), on a specific status update or content element (such as images or links to a brand's website), or on event invites. One tactic Facebook leverages is showing a sampling of a participant's network who likes a page to encourage others to join in "liking" the page. This tactic is related to the use of reference groups, examined in the next section. In Figure 3.6, Netflix shows a participant's friend who likes the brand and presents a call to action leading to a website landing page promoting exclusive streaming video content.[18]

Sponsored content takes the form of a regular brand update on a person's social network feed; however, sponsored content does not come

Figure 3.6 A member of your network "likes Netflix"

Figure 3.7 Twitter marks paid tweets as "promoted"

from brands subscribed for by the user. In this case, the brand paid the social media platform for its content to appear in the feed. This approach is used by both Twitter (denoted as Promoted) and Facebook (denoted as Sponsored), as can be seen in Figures 3.6 and 3.7.

On Twitter, sponsored tweets appear toward the top of the Twitter stream and indicate sponsored content with an orange arrow, like this update from e-mail administrator Mailchimp.[19]

Twitter also allows sponsored user suggestions, which prompt participants to follow an account that has paid to be suggested, and Twitter sells access to its trending keywords.

Relevance of the Message

Research in traditional advertising has established the need to create and communicate a relevant message to the target consumer base. Social media communication requires the same level of relevance and consistency. As previously mentioned, brand messages and endorsements shared by reference groups (a group that an individual perceives to be similar to himself or herself) are also important in social media. Types of social media exposure that consumers encounter vary greatly and include status updates, paid advertising units, sponsored stories (advertising), implied endorsements, and location check-ins. In visual networks, such as Pinterest and Instagram, exposures include image sharing by users or resharing of another user's images.

As with all forms of marketing communication, messages must be relevant to the intended audience. This tenet holds true in social media, where the goal is to foster a long-term relationship and ongoing two-way communication. If a brand's message, including images, web links, consumer testimonials, and video content, is not relevant to consumers, then brand community cannot be fostered. Consumers can unsubscribe from a brand as easily as they originally followed the brand. It is critical for brands to closely monitor key social media metrics, such as new followers, unsubcribes, and (if available) the number of followers who muted or hid the brand from their feed. These measures provide a critical barometer for whether the message is on target and which posts generate the most activity. Engagement with posts, including sharing and endorsements (such as likes on Facebook or retweets on Twitter), provides further corroboration that the content created and shared by a brand is on target.

When a message is relevant and the delivery is passionate, that relevance leads to resonance, which can *create* mass influence. Social media tools offer new ways for brands to increase perceived relevance for consumers. The relevance of social media is the degree to which the media is perceived as identity relevant. Simply put, psychological research has shown that consumers foster and maintain a number of situational-specific identities, and media consumed can be shown to positively contribute to a person's identity. A history of consuming identity-relevant media enables the consumer's identity and provides behavioral evidence that informs self-attributions about identity importance. In the brand social network, live and authentic messages are important, and these messages must resonate with the target audience.

Relevance of the Reference Group

A reference group is any group of people that an individual identifies with and uses to form attitudes and guide behaviors. For college students, fellow students within the same major may serve as a reference group. For professionals, people in the same discipline, such as nursing, can serve as a reference group. In all cases, individuals look to their reference group for signals about appropriate behavior, attitudes, and values. The relevance of the reference group is an important factor when considering how social media interactions influence identification with other brand fans and the importance of the brand relationship to the consumer's identity. In the social network, ties can range from weak to strong, and reference groups must be relevant in order to significantly influence behavior. If a social media exposure occurs with a friend or a member of a relevant reference group, the rate of identification will be higher than if the reference group is not relevant.[20] This concept has been demonstrated with research showing that when consumers are shown rapid images with brand logos discreetly placed in context of the photo, brand choice was influenced by the logos presented. Half of the participants were shown images of individuals wearing clothing with brand logos likely to prime the participants for the reference group (college logo of their school). The other half were shown images of individuals wearing clothing with logos not likely to prime the reference group (college logo from a different school). Participants were more likely to choose brands shown when the images primed the participant's reference group.[21] When users of social media encounter a brand interaction, such as someone liking a page, commenting positively about a brand, or checking into a location and sharing this update, the observer is likely to judge the brand more favorably when they perceive the endorsers to be part of their reference group. Consumers are typically more favorable toward content endorsed by their perceived reference group.

While Facebook uses the nomenclature of "Friend," the composition of an online social network, in reality, is a continuum that spans from strangers to acquaintances to lifelong friends to family. Early in Facebook's history of display advertising, the newsfeed would show a brand's ad with a list of friends who liked the brand. What Facebook did not consider was whether or not the user actually considered the endorsers part of their social network. In this scenario, if the user did not consider the network members chosen by Facebook to be part of his or her reference group, the user would not look as favorably upon the brand message as he or she would if the endorsers had been friends. This puts Facebook at risk for the undesirable consequences of negative brand associations.

Facebook has taken steps to improve its ability to predict the nature of the relationship between the individuals in the network and, thus, how endorsements of sponsored content and display ads affect others. When a Facebook member adds a new friend or accepts a friend request, Facebook now asks whether the member knows this person offline. This information contributes to Facebook's repository on the relationship of the member for better online ad targeting. Also, Facebook tracks which members of a participant's network are frequently engaged online with the participant (or conversely has muted or hidden). This information is appended to Facebook's database of member relations, called Facebook Graph. Understanding the complex nature of online friendships allows Facebook to know who would qualify as a "frenemy" versus a "friend" and monitor weak ties versus strong ties. Facebook is able to present better brand-sponsored ads when the reference group is better defined.

The mobile social network Foursquare also uses the concept of the reference group when making location suggestions to users (Figure 3.8). Foursquare does not appear to maintain knowledge of the interactions between participants. This is most likely because as a location-sharing platform, it is highly unlikely that a user would allow frenemies, acquaintances, and strangers to know his or her location. A suggestion on Foursquare shows a thumbnail of a person in the user's network that has visited a location and the frequency of visits. In Figure 3.8, five thumbnails are shown that indicate who in the network has visited that location. Hovering over a thumbnail on the web version of Foursquare shows the frequency.[22]

Consumers make judgments based on knowledge of congruency between their own preferences and those of their network. When users

Figure 3.8 Foursquare's use of the reference group

perceive parallels between their own tastes and those of contacts shown, a favorable evaluation is likely to occur. Further, recent academic research has found that relevance of the reference group impacts a consumer's judgment of that brand on Facebook.[23] This research indicates that hiding or revealing the demographic characteristics of a brand's fans can positively or negatively influence evaluations of the brand by others. Thus, consumers are likely to make positive judgments when content is relevant and when the person generating the content is someone the user identifies with.

Case Study: Neiman Marcus

For a unique look into the strategic execution of social media, we look to upscale retailer Neiman Marcus.[24] The retailer has pages for its main brand and individual pages for its specific stores, with the highest number of social media followers being on the Facebook page. Neiman Marcus's main Facebook page had over 850,000 active users in 2015.[25] However, primary interaction takes place on other networks. For example, the brand has earned over 82,000 followers on Pinterest,[26] and each piece of visual content actually gets more engagement than posts on Facebook. Pinterest users can both endorse a visual image or "repin" it to their own profile's boards. The brand curates a number of boards with the theme "The Art of." Topics within this theme include "The Art of Giving," "The Art of Words," and "The Art of Black and White." These boards highlight topics related to various categories of Neiman Marcus products.

With over 300,000 followers, the brand enjoys high per post engagement on Instagram.[27] While the number of total followers is a fraction of that of Neiman Marcus's Facebook followers, the total engagement per post is the highest of all of the networks on which the brand participates. Figure 3.9 contains a post featuring a merchandise window for the holiday season. This post received over 3,000 endorsements from Instagram users, which is far more successful than the fewer than 100 endorsements per Facebook post the brand receives.[28]

Figure 3.9 Neiman Marcus enjoys high interaction from consumers

Note that while the execution of the social media content may look seamless to the observer, creating social media content is quite multifaceted for a brand as complex as Neiman Marcus. With many locations throughout the United States, regional tastes and variations must be taken into account. The public relations group that directs social media activities for the brand has designed a well-planned strategy that allows various stores to create and contribute content for use across social media channels. Regular training on topics such as brand tone and appealing photos is provided to key contacts at stores so that consistency is possible. The result is a mix of text content and images that reflect the diverse fashions and trends available through the retail chain. The firm also takes a "test and learn" approach to the ever-changing social media landscape. Neiman Marcus was an early pioneer in mobile social networks, running early promotions with location network SCVNGR. They were also an early adopter of Vine, featuring six-second "sizzle" reels from New York Fashion Week. While Neiman Marcus is a massive operation with a niche, upscale audience, the retailer's willingness to test and learn in an effort to find the optimal social media footprint (while sourcing content from each of its regions) is best practice. Had the brand stuck with social media exemplars Facebook and Twitter, they would have missed opportunities to exploit smaller social media platforms (i.e., Pinterest and Instagram) where they have engaged more consumers per post.

Figure 3.10 Neiman Marcus appeals to consumers via Pinterest

Key Takeaways

- Many types of brand exposure opportunities exist; some are generated by the brand, but the most powerful exposures come from peer-to-peer brand discussions.
- Consumers make judgments on both the relevance of the message about the brand and the people who associate themselves with the brand in social media, known as a reference group.
- Consumers weigh whether or not consumer-generated content comes from people like them or from someone not like them.
- Research shows that when advertising messages, including social media, show a reference group relevant to the observer, a more favorable judgment is likely to be elicited in the observer.
- While image- and video-based social networks such as Instagram, Vine, and Pinterest may be smaller than Facebook, their content can be spread through the larger networks. Brands must decide on an optimal social media footprint.
- Visual networks, like Instagram, Pinterest, and Vine, may result in higher referral traffic to e-commerce sites. While Facebook is a mandatory due to its critical mass of active users, more effort may be warranted on smaller networks.

- Monitoring return on investment through metrics such as referral traffic, sales conversions, and e-mail signups should serve as a barometer for where to focus efforts.
- Social media customer service is a mandatory; consumers expect that you will respond to them, and consumers observing the actions of a brand (or inaction) assume the brand will treat them the same in the future.
- Resolving a customer service issue in social media is more than asking them to call the call center; most likely they tried and gave up. Find ways to push them into a chat conversation, like @askamex does in their Card Center section of the website.
- Resolved issues can result in raving fans. Good word of mouth from resolved issues reinforces the brand's story online.
- Test and learn. There is no one size fits all solution in social media. Try new content across various networks to see what engages brand fans effectively.
- Snapchat is a growing way to reach younger mobile users through video.

CHAPTER 4

Community Characteristics

Building Brand Identification

Brand identification is considered a critical predecessor for building brand community. Advertising research encourages brands to become relevant for their target consumer base. Social media provides a platform wherein consumers seek brands relevant to their self-concept and, therefore, build personal identification with those brands. In addition, brand endorsements shared by consumers' reference groups (people they identify with or aspire to) further enhance the consumer tendency to build identification with a brand and its products. The types of social media brand endorsements that consumers may encounter varies greatly, and includes status updates, paid advertising units, sponsored stories (native advertising), implied endorsements, and location check-ins. In visual networks such as Pinterest and Instagram, exposures can include image sharing by a user or the resharing of another user's images.

Brand Identification

Identification is a form of psychological bonding between individuals and brands.[1] As mentioned in the previous discussion of brand experiences, brands reflect specific values and traits that individuals consider central to their identity.[2] This affective attachment leads to identification with a particular brand, making that brand stand out in the consumer's mind relative to all others in the marketplace.

Greater identification with a brand leads to enhanced familiarity and distinctive brand associations.[3] Brand identification is necessary for consumers to be open to brand experiences and brand-related social media. Online interaction in brand communities leads to a consciousness of shared rituals and traditions.[4] Strong brand identification is likely when brands have developed prominent characteristics and consumers perceive the brand to be providing value.[5] Brand identification is considered a critical predecessor for consumers who wish to be a part of the online brand community.

For a community to form once brand identity is realized, there are important relational factors to consider: the consumer must have experiences with the brand, the consumer needs to be exposed to social media related to the brand, and opportunities for social networking need to be available. Community formation is most likely to occur when the community group and brand messages are relevant to both the consumer and the group. Once formed, brand communities are held together by the sense of community that emerges from these shared interests.

To further solidify consumers' identification with a brand (and building enduring bonds that can lead to the ultimate goal of brand community), social media exposure to the brand and its brand fans is necessary. Social media exposure can take many forms, depending on the social network in use. Social media vary in execution and primary content type. For instance, Facebook is a mixture of both images and text, while Twitter is a 140-character microblog that is heavily text-based; Pinterest and Instagram allow participants to share user-generated images or reshare the content of other participants.

Brand communities are made up of members who form relationships, which often lead to emotional bonds.[6] Many communities exist based on identification with a brand developed through a significant consumption experience. From the customer experience perspective, brand community is a fabric of relationships in which the customer is situated. Crucial relationships include those: (1) between the customer and the brand, (2) between the customer and the firm, (3) between the customer and the product, and (4) among fellow customers. Academic research on brand community has traditionally focused on niche (e.g., Jeep) or luxury brands (e.g., Mercedes). However, the notion of brand community has been extended to convenience products (e.g., Nutella).[7] For consumers who strongly support a brand like Nutella, social media channels provide an easy, effective way to organize their brand efforts. For instance, World Nutella Day, a fan organized event, boasts over 42,000 fans and is not organized or endorsed by the Nutella brand.[8]

Figure 4.1 Armie Hammer embarks on a Vespa Adventure

Consumer-created campaigns are not the norm. A more common way to facilitate community is through the creation of social media accounts (such as branded Facebook pages, Twitter accounts, Instagram channels, etc.). Through these channels, brands initiate conversations with brand fans, and brand fans interact with the brand as well as other consumers who share a passion for the brand. Content driving conversations is experiential and reinforces the brand. For instance, well-known actor Armie Hammer embarked on a journey across the United States sponsored by Vespa. Vespa documented his journey on its social channels, including Twitter, Facebook, and the branded online community La Vespa Vita (Figure 4.1). As the actor crossed the United States, images reinforced the carefree Italian spirit the brand holds as a core value.[9]

Our conceptual model is rooted in social identity theory, which explores the importance of identities to the overall self-concept; identity is the single most important predictor of sustained behaviors.[10] Identity theory emphasizes how using brands, symbols, and enacting-behaviors contributes to one's self-concept. In the following sections, we discuss how brand identification, identification with others, and identity salience impact how consumers behave.

Identification with Others

Consumers share experiences to enhance their bond with others based on their passion for a brand and company.[11] Staging activities and events that encourage fan interaction facilitates this bond. The American motorcycle brand Harley Davidson invites community members to take a pilgrimage to meet and interact with other Harley owners, while Vespa shares the journey of Armie Hammer via brand updates on social media. For Harley owners, taking the journey reinforces the user experience and brand image. Vespa hopes that experiencing the journey vicariously will have the same effect for its consumers. Through interaction with both the product and other consumers, a sense of community is developed. We consider these participants to be connected consumers, in that they are connected with the brand and other community members through digital technology. These connected consumers associate with not only the brand, but also other owners who share the road, locally and across the world. As brands continue to play an important role in consumers' purchasing decisions, brand community helps to identify the perceived social image of consumers.[12]

An emerging interaction between consumers and brands comes in the form of interactions with company executives via social media. Prior to the open nature of social media interactions, the average consumer would rarely have the opportunity to interact with firm executives. However, as firm executives become de facto spokespeople for the brand in social media, this is changing. Perceived access to executives further enhances consumer bonds with companies, brands, and products.

At the 2014 Consumer Electronic Show (CES) in Las Vegas, T-Mobile CEO John Legere crashed the AT&T developer party featuring a performance by Macklemore & Ryan Lewis. After entering the event with no problems, he was unceremoniously thrown out of the party by security after a photo of him at the event was tweeted.[13] This event resulted in several additional tweets about his ejection and significant press attention to the heated competition between the two carriers. In T-Mobile's own CES event, it was announced that the carrier would pay contract break fees for any new mobile customer defecting from a competitor, namely AT&T, Sprint, and Verizon. Consumers taking advantage of the offer tweeted CEO John Legere about their "breakup" experiences with switching carriers. The tweets were accompanied with the hashtag #breakupletters, which Legere gleefully retweeted. In Figure 4.2, a new customer poses with his T-Mobile purchases and a defaced Verizon logo,

Sample Customer @newcustomer   21h
@newcustomer Breaking up never felt so good! #breakupletters
#uncarrier @TMobile pic.twitter.com/T00SR0Iy6h
Retweeted by

Expand

Figure 4.2 A Verizon customer defects publically to T-Mobile via Twitter

which was retweeted by John Legere to his followers.[14] Social media now provides more ways to interact with the brand and allows consumers to feel part of the larger community, including validation by corporate executives.

Identity Salience

Research related to identity salience is vast. Consumers embrace brands participating in online communities based on the strength and relevance of the identification. The simplest explanation for this is that consumers have multiple identities they take on in daily life, which, together, comprise what researchers call the "total self." For example, a consumer may be a working mother of three with heavy involvement in philanthropic endeavors. Each of those roles (mother, working professional, philanthropist) is an identity the consumer embraces, and together they form the identity of the individual. Identities vary in salience and importance to the total self. This differential salience influences how consumers adapt their self-presentation to others, both offline and via social media. The level of a specific role's salience is the single most essential predictor of sustained role-related behaviors.[15] In simple terms, more salient roles (or identities) better predict behaviors of individuals. What leads to higher identity salience? Identity theory emphasizes how self-definition arises. Consumers self-define themselves more by ongoing social interactions and communications instead of the larger social structure within which they operate. This tendency to focus on salient interactions and communications for defining their own identities is a form of symbolic interactionism. The tenets of symbolic interactionism suggest that ongoing communications throughout a consumer's daily life, such as interactions with friends, strangers, online brands, and brand communities, contribute to an individual's perception of himself or herself. Hence, the relevance of the reference group and the relevance of the message influence how consumers identify with others and how important the relationship with the brand is to the identity of a person. Social relationships related to salient identities fuel self-attributions and thus lead to modified behavior.

This somewhat dense discussion of self and the varying importance of micro-interactions with those in a person's network can be simplified. Brand relationships vary in strength and importance; some hold greater personal meaning than others. A beloved hotel that was visited on a honeymoon would hold greater importance (and contribute to a consumer's identity) than the consumer's electric company (with which the consumer would interact with on a more regular basis through daily utility service, bill receipt, bill payment, etc.). Because the hotel held an emotional meaning to the consumer and perhaps activated the consumer's sense of romance and adventure, it would hold higher importance to the utility service. Social media interaction likely follows this trend. Consumers are more likely to interact with brands and remain brand loyal when the emotional bond is salient.

Brand Community

When we use the term brand community, it transcends interaction through social media. Consumers feel a sense of attachment to the brand, beyond what would form through simple forum interactions (like a customer service forum). Formation of brand community means that consumers have forged a deeper bond with the brand than casual consumers have formed, and they actively and consciously embrace that brand and its fellow supporters. In the context of this book, consumers interact with each other through social media. Three elements must exist for a brand community to form: (1) "consciousness of kind," meaning one consumer recognizes another as being like-minded, (2) shared rituals, meaning individuals perform social acts specific to the brand experience that only others within the group understand, and (3) consumer interactions, either in person or online.[16] Consumers identify with the brand and with other consumers of the brand. This identification leads to strong bonds, a sense of kinship, an atmosphere of trust, community-specific rituals, and a shared culture. Thus, identification with the brand and identification with others who identify with the brand lead to a formation of brand community. Marketers would be well served to develop this community of devoted, loyal, and fervent consumers. When consumers interact in a community, there are interactions and shared feelings that lead to identification with others in the community. Consumers learn to identify with the brand through brand characteristics and relational factors. Identification with the brand and owners is positively related to brand community.

Examples of Brand Community and Identity Salience

One type of interaction on brand social media channels is shared content by consumers. In this case, content, such as images, video, or text testimonials, show a commitment to other brand supporters and to the brand. For example, fans of the smart watch Pebble, a wearable device that displays push notifications from smartphones, post photos of their newly received devices or creative photography of their devices in use. In the example below, a Pebble fan photographed his device and shared with Pebble on its Facebook page (shown in Figure 4.3).[17]

Figure 4.3 Photograph of Pebble shared with the Facebook community

When consumers share their user experiences and affinity for a brand, they conspicuously signify to other current and potential consumers that the product is of high quality, worth the cost, deserving of their loyalty, and an important part of who they are. Additionally, as social media is social by nature, shared content with an online brand community also provides incidental exposure to the network of the community member. Through incidental exposure, clues to the consumers' identity salience with the brand are exposed to the community at large.

Key Takeaways

- Brand community is much more than consumers participating on a brand's Facebook page; consumers feel a deeper connection to the brand, and their "membership" may signify a badge of honor or association.
- Interactions with other brand owners matter; there is a shared kinship that comes from ownership, such as the Vespa owners sharing their favorite ride images.
- Interactions with the brand can also include company executives, which is a recent development facilitated by social media.
- Consumers have multiple identities based on the roles they hold in their daily lives; these identities vary in importance, and the day-to-day interactions help predict the future behaviors as part of these identities. In short, consumers are complex and malleable in various aspects of their lives.
- Brand relationships reinforce identities, and sharing the ownership or consumption of a beloved brand reinforces identity salience.
- Content shared with the brand and fellow brand supporters on social media signals membership in the community and reinforces its contribution to the consumer's identity.

- Brands wishing to form brand community must truly think of their social media efforts as a community forum. This is not advertising, but a community shared by consumers and facilitated by the brand.
- When brands facilitate brand interactions with meaningful content and kinship between their consumers, traditional one-to-many advertising messages are transcended.

CHAPTER 5

Virtually There

Online Versus Face-to-Face Brand Communities

Academic brand community research has primarily focused on shared rituals and face-to-face gatherings of brand fans. With the widespread adoption of social media, brand supporters can share in virtual live gatherings via images shared on Facebook pages, YouTube streaming of live events, Vine video vignettes summarizing brand gatherings, descriptions in blogs, and a myriad other medium. While a face-to-face brand gathering, like a Harley Davidson bike rally, can create a strong emotional bond and positive memories for participants, social media allows a consumer to share in the experience from a distance. In this chapter, we discuss three successful online brand gatherings. These virtual gatherings allow community members to join in from afar. These examples are from the following brands: the fashion brand DKNY, Apple iOS, and Downton Abbey, a television show with a large following.

Case Study 1: DKNY

The Virtual Pajama Party

Fashion brand DKNY made social media a hallmark of its marketing and communications efforts for years. In an unusual strategy, the brand once featured two different "voices" in social media. On Facebook, Instagram, and Pinterest, the voice of the brand was DKNY, while on Twitter and the brand's Tumblr blog, the voice was that of their SVP Global Communications at Donna Karan International, in the form of the @dkny PR Girl Persona. From this Twitter handle, information concerning the daily operations of DKNY public relations were shared tweeted to brand fans and followers. This type of content provided an insider view of the craziness of fashion PR and allowed fans to feel a deeper sense of connection with the brand and the DKNY executive. Through these channels, @dkny PR Girl documented both the fun and frustrating challenges running the brand's communications, including popular postings about unreasonable fashion show seating requests from journalists and wannabe journalists.

The original execution of the DKNY PR Girl was that of a nameless public relations employee providing insider access, and the identity of the voice was not known by most followers. The creator of this content, the DKNY PR Girl, was portrayed as a fashionable avatar that reflected the current season and DKNY fashions. Over time, it became more difficult for the executive behind DKNY PR Girl to separate her personality from that of the online persona.[1] To lift the veil, the woman behind the tweets, Aliza Licht, released a YouTube video entitled "The Real DKNY PR Girl." Her video provided insight into DKNY's communication strategy and social media, including Licht's real identity.[2] This move to out herself on social media has led to many opportunities to enhance the DKNY brand as well as Licht's own brand.

Licht's activity under the DKNY social media accounts included unique activities not often undertaken by branded social media accounts. For example, she frequently live tweeted television shows known to be popular with DKNY's fan base including *Revenge, Gossip Girl,* and *Scandal.* While no formal partnership exists between the brand and these entertainment properties, the DKNY account interacted with fans and stars of these television shows each week. These hour-long sessions allowed brand fans to interact with a company executive about topics completely unrelated to marketing the DKNY product. With over 483,000 followers during this approach to social media, these Twitter viewing parties become a virtual pajama party.

Licht also hosted viewing parties online during the major entertainment awards shows, including the Golden Globes, Screen Actors Guild Awards, and Academy Awards (Oscars). During her live tweets of red carpet events, her brand fans (who she refers to as friends and not followers) were given insight as to the brand's efforts to dress celebrities for the events. By describing the anticipation of seeing "Celeb X" walking the red carpet in Donna Karan Atelier (the couture brand), Licht shared the brand's victories (and sometime disappointment when Celeb X has switched to a competitor brand last minute). Brand fans were encouraged to share these images on their own Tumblr blogs or other social media channels. Fashion brands depend on word of mouth to drive interest in their brands and collections, and DKNY built a faithful following during this era. These fans were not only loyal to the brand but also to the executive behind the voice of the brand.

In addition to the informal TV viewing parties and the awards show live tweeting, DKNY also used social media channels to broadcast its major fashion shows (before the launch of Periscope and other broadcasting applications). While journalists covet the seats at the live events (and jockey for the best seats), brand fans sat front row via live streaming. Additionally, brand community participants received live commentary directly from Licht, who live tweeted during the show while performing her other duties. During the event, brand community members commented and tweeted as the models worked their way down the runway.

Additionally, DKNY recruited brand community members to tweet as part of campaign launches. The brand used community members as the stars of the viral video content. This approach validated brand community members' participation and encourages word-of-mouth communication; members who were featured shared this video and details of the campaign with their networks and shared the information offline with their expanded network of friends and family. While academic brand community research considers offline brand gatherings as the exemplar interaction, these virtual pajama parties and inclusive online approach for events big and small provide an inexpensive way for the brand community to interact with the voice of the brand in a low-pressure, inviting environment on a regular basis. This investment in brand fan interactions, for both DKNY events and non-brand events like television show discussions, proved worth the time and effort as measured by fan count and engagement with the brand. These approaches are authentic and encourage involvement. Additionally, when brand community members take an active role in championing a brand, they develop a deeper investment in the brand and community.

In August 2015, DKNY deleted all social media content from Twitter and Tumblr as originated by Licht's DKNY PR Girl.[3] Following the departure of founder Donna Karan and other top execs, the brand shifted creative direction. Additionally, all fans and friends of the @dkny Twitter account were promptly unfollowed in the course of a single day. Basically, the relationships built and the visual and text history of the rich brand community created and fostered by Licht were deleted in a day. While it's not uncommon for new creative leaders to want to make their own mark on a brand's identity, erasing years of history and the digital artifacts of relationships painstakingly created by Licht seems very shortsighted and antithetical to the concept of fostering brand community via social media. What once was visually and tonally unique to DKNY now sat as an empty Twitter page and an Instagram account indistinguishable from other mainstream designers. In short, the brand euthanized not only the DKNY PR Girl persona but also the spirit and strategy of brand community fostered over years and thousands of personal interactions.

For her part, Licht has proven to be a successful curator of compelling content and a master community builder. After the content was deleted from the DKNY account, Licht and the brand announced her departure from the firm.[4] Based on the success of her career guidance book *Leave Your Mark: Land Your Dream Job. Kill It in Your Career. Rock Social Media*, Licht saw considerable demand for her expertise in the media and speaking events. As expected, the community she built under the DKNY have followed her to her personal account, and she now serves as an online mentor to thousands. The same events she would tweet for the brand are now tweeted via her personal account. This is an example of when a transparent and authentic executive's community building is not only effective in building community but also in creating personal relationships that survive separation from the brand.

Case Study 2: Apple iOS Devices

A different approach to brand community is executed by followers and supporters of Apple's mobile devices, the iPhone and iPad product lines (collectively known as iOS devices). Apple has not invested resources into the traditional online community for its devices; for example, no official

Facebook page exists for iPhone. However, a user-generated Facebook page has been created for iPhone with over 14 million followers as of June 2014.[5] This page imports Wikipedia information and shows groups and pages related to iPhone. Apple invested in a music-centric community known as Ping, which went virtually ignored by iTunes users. This failure to build a successful community led Apple to discontinue the Ping community in 2013.[6] New Apple product launches and the proceeding rumors are closely tied to where and when Apple users join in the brand community. For months, rumors were shared through the media that Apple planned a product in the wearable category,[7] which was confirmed at a media event.[8] Depending on the importance of the event, Apple may live stream the event or allow keynote speakers to be viewed online or via Apple devices (such as Apple TV) afterward. The audience members who are invited to the event are not passive participants; they actively tweet, live blog, and post updates of the event as new details are revealed. Technology blogs such as Engadget, The Unofficial Apple Weblog, TechCrunch, and others run stories that automatically update with images of the keynote slides and presenters so that readers can follow along. Figure 5.1 shows the live blogging and images posted during the launch of Apple iPhone 5s.[9]

These updates are shared real-time on Twitter, and Apple fans can follow. While Apple lacks a firm presence in social media, brand

Figure 5.1 Engadget liveblog of Apple iPhone 5s and 5c announcements

community members share news and updates as empowered by the technology blogs. Forrester Research's NetBase unit measured the number of mentions surrounding the launch of the iPhone 5s and 5c. Days prior to the event, Twitter mentions of "iPhone" hovered below 10,000 mentions per day, likely elevated from normal due to the run-up to the event.[10] The day of the event, over 110,000 mentions of the device occurred on Twitter, indicating that Twitter participants were sharing news and interacting with one another about the event.

Case Study 3: Downton Abbey

Tea, Tiaras, and Twitter: The Social TV Phenomenon

Before 2012, the typical television viewer likely would associate public television network PBS with such serious programs as Nova, News-Hour, and childrens' programming like Sesame Street or Mr. Rogers. However, a British import for the PBS Mainstay Masterpiece changed this perception, becoming both a ratings hit and social media phe-nomenon. The story of the upper-class Crawley family, led by the Earl of Grantham, captivated viewers. Its large following has resulted in a community on Twitter that converses via tweets while viewing the show. According to Nielsen Social Guide, 97,000 tweets were generated during the U.S. Season 4 premiere. These tweets resulted in 15.2 million total impressions for the show, and the telecast ranked second for the day (excluding sports).[11] For a show on PBS to reach this level of buzz and social media consumption would be unthinkable in the past. In addition to the organic discussion surrounding the #DowntonPBS topic hashtag, PBS has driven conversation with popular bloggers such as Tom and Lorenzo (@tomandlorenzo on Twitter),[12] entertainment journalists such as Jarett Wieselman of Buzzfeed, celebrity fan Patton Oswalt, and stars from the series. Figure 5.2 shows a tweet from the @tomandlorenzo Twitter feed.

PBS has taken the additional step of heavily promoting the #DowntonPBS hashtag in integrated marketing efforts, such as Downton Abbey-branded social media campaigns, backgrounds, and banners, as illustrated in the Twitter background shown in Figure 5.3.[13]

Figure 5.2 Live tweets from bloggers Tom + Lorenzo

Figure 5.3 Celebrity Patton Oswalt's Downton tweets on branded Twitter wallpaper

As with many aspects of popular culture, the show has spawned a number of social media parodies, including the voluble tribute to protagonist Lady Mary's eyebrows on Twitter (@L_MarysEyebrows).[14] Social media channels have responded to the inherent social nature of television viewing and provide a shared audience with which fans can share emotional reactions to events on the show. Most sites support hashtags, which allow participants to search updates related to the topic or show of interest. Additionally, Facebook has added a feature related to what the user is doing, such as watching television. Now-defunct mobile application tvtag (formerly GetGlue) performed a similar feature, where users can "check in" to shows and syndicate that activity as an update on social networks like Facebook and Twitter. Because of the ongoing dialogue around television shows, social conversation and check-ins are now taken into account when reporting the success of a television show.

Nielsen, traditionally known for measuring television ratings, launched Nielsen SocialGuide to add the element of social discussion into television ratings. For each ranked episode, Nielsen reports the number of tweets associated with a television show, the number of unique authors or Tweeters, the number of impressions, and unique audience.[15] Per Nielsen, for every Twitter participant tweeting about a television show, 50 brand exposures occur for that show.[16] In the challenging television market where shows are given little time to catch on or face cancellation, driving word of mouth for TV franchises is mandatory for network executives. Additionally, Nielsen has started conducting new research to establish causality between tweets and viewership, which will further justify investment in social media brand community for television franchises as these findings are further corroborated.[17] For a time, mobile application tvtag published real-time trending television viewership on its mobile app and website, and total check-ins are cited in media publications such as AdAge.[18] In Figure 5.4, real-time viewing statistics reflect the shows that tvtag viewers have indicated they are currently watching; a mid-afternoon snapshot captures primetime TV shows Arrow and Supernatural (likely viewed by DVR) and daytime dramas General Hospital and The Young and the Restless (likely viewed real time).[19] Using this service as additional insight, media and broadcast organizations gained insight into which shows are valuable enough to viewers to share with their networks (and strangers) through social media. While the service has been discontinued, it is reasonable

Figure 5.4 tvtag mobile social real-time check-in tracking

to expect a similar service to fill the void it left. Additionally, Facebook now includes a "watching" status to share the consumption of TV and entertainment content with a participant's network.

Key Takeaways

- Traditional brand communities have focused on face-to-face events, while online brand communities in social media can participate remotely in brand events.
- Events can include product-related events or peripheral activities, such as DKNY's live tweeting of TV shows popular with its community.
- Including brand community members in advertising efforts drives deeper engagement with the brand and has built in word of mouth.
- While brand rallies such as Harley Davidson group rides were the standard for brand gatherings, online brand gatherings are gaining traction (such as the cross-country Vespa rally).
- Social media brand community also facilitates word of mouth and buzz related to popular television programming. Traditional social media channels like Twitter and Facebook are augmented with mobile smartphone apps such as tvtag.
- Social conversation and check-ins have a multiplier effect on exposure, and traditional media measurement organization Nielsen has responded by launching conversation measurement. It behooves network executives to embrace social media and allocate resources to fostering authentic conversation.
- Unlikely social media darling PBS's Downton Abbey demonstrates that social media conversations and community can form far beyond brands and can encourage adoption and consumption of atypical television programming.

- Geography no longer limits brand community; from the comfort of the participant's living room, brand community interaction can occur anywhere (like @dkny's virtual pajama party on awards nights or appointment television viewings).
- Once a brand has built relationships through thousands of interactions, it is shortsighted to delete that content just because of new management or creative direction. The consumers who cocreated the content may feel alienated or disconnected from the brand.

CHAPTER 6

The Nature of Fandom and Shared Power in the Social Environment

Participating in a brand community has no barriers to entry; anyone can join in a brand conversation on social media channels. Not every brand fan will engage in consumption of the product. In the marketing literature, repeat purchase is equivalent to loyalty and requires brand managers to rethink the metrics they use to define brand success. Loyalty is defined as "a deeply held commitment to rebuy or repatronize a preferred product or service consistently in the future, thereby causing repetitive same-brand or same brand-set purchasing, despite situational influences and marketing efforts having the potential to cause switching behavior."[1] For necessity products, consumers repeat purchase for very different reasons than for other types of products, particularly luxury goods. High involvement product categories are relevant to the consumers' sense of self. Brand communities are formed around products that are important to consumers.[2] It is logical to assume that low involvement purchases such as home utilities likely do not result in brand community (in fact, any social media feedback will likely be negative due to lack of consumer alternatives). For brands that are relevant to consumers, participants engage with brands in social media as a foreshadowing of future purchase. In some cases fandom is solely aspirational and purchase is unlikely. In this case the brand may align with the consumer's values but price prevents purchase for this particular consumer. Aspirational consumers play a unique role in the brand community as they serve to increase the confidence of owners of the brand and push those who are on the cusp of owning to strive for the future purchase.

Brands directed messages at consumers in the business relationship with one-way communication. With social media, this balance has clearly tipped the other direction. When consumers were dissatisfied they complained to the company. This negative word-of-mouth communication was face-to-face with family, friends, and neighbors. Today, however, consumers share their dissatisfaction on social media and have a much wider audience. Factors affecting the reach of word-of-mouth communication have fundamentally changed. If a brand is not monitoring the discussion in social media channels and participating in the discussion, they miss opportunities to position their brand effectively with the most influential consumers. Staying ever-present on social media and monitoring the state of the brand means resolving customer service issues publicly so that solving one person's problem becomes an opportunity to gain brand fans. Consumers use rating sites such as Yelp, TripAdvisor, and Google Places as an integrated network with social media channels such as Twitter, YouTube, and Facebook to find recommendations, interact with brands, and offer tips to others. Any consumer armed with a smartphone can record video and images of a positive or negative service encounter and share with his or her extended network in social media; in many cases, these encounters go viral.

In this chapter, we explore the differences between fans and consumers of a brand. Furthermore, we explore alternative strategies brands may pursue to convert brand fans to brand consumers. We also explore the common phenomenon of consumer feedback via social media and ways the brand can turn negative encounters into positive experiences with the brand. Finally, we discuss an emerging phenomenon of informal brand ambassadors, where consumers intervene in social media to help resolve customer experience issues.

Why Fans May Not Be Consumers

Brand loyalty encompasses both purchase loyalty and attitudinal loyalty.[3] Although managers frequently measure repeat purchase and purchase intent to predict brand loyalty, it is only one component of consumer loyalty. Brands have wide fan bases ranging from consumers with ultimate loyalty—a consumer who is loyal against all odds. As already mentioned, aspiring consumers may possess strong attitudinal loyalty toward a brand.

These consumers may never purchase a brand's product or may purchase only once in a lifetime (depending on the cost point). However, they remain psychologically committed to the brand.

One brand family with a vast fan base is Virgin. Virgin's portfolio contains more than 50 distinct business units. Within those are brands within the entertainment, health and wellness, leisure, financial, telecom and tech, travel, and sustainability industries.[4] From Virgin Mobile to global airlines, consumers have the opportunity to become brand fans across a number of product categories. This affinity for one brand does not imply that consumers are true prospective consumers for all of the Virgin brands. A U.S. consumer may be a frequent flyer for Virgin America, but it is unlikely he or she will ever be a customer for the Virgin Galactic brand. Virgin Galactic provides the service of space flight and weightlessness to adventurous consumers. Consumers fly in a glider that piggybacks on a mother ship. Once at the edge of the Earth's atmosphere, the glider separates and provides passengers with a unique, out of this world experience. The price point (over $200,000 per flight) for Virgin Galactic's services is likely to be too high for many of Virgin's brand fans. However, even those consumers who will never experience space flight on Virgin Galactic possess psychological affinity toward the company and its services because of their existing affinity for the Virgin brand. As shown in Figure 6.1, Virgin Galactic has over 70,000 followers on Twitter, a number that far exceeds the number of actual purchasers for its services.

Figure 6.1 Virgin Galactic communicates with a community of 70,000+ followers on Twitter

While over 70,000 consumers follow Virgin Galactic on Twitter as of February 2014, most of these consumers will never convert to consumers of the brand. However, the brand does have products or services that are more accessible to consumers. The Virgin family brand ranges from Virgin Galactic to Virgin Mobile. The consumer may follow Virgin Galactic but gain entry into the brand through Virgin Mobile. While Virgin Mobile prepaid mobile phone service is an easy, cost-effective entry into the Virgin brand family, a seat on Virgin Galactic costs $250,000 per seat (six per flight) for a 2.5-hour flight with six minutes of weightlessness. Following the brand may signal support of the Virgin brand, identification with the brand, or aspirations for future experiences like the space flight (despite a lack of economic means to fund the desired experience). This fan base helps raise awareness of Virgin and its family of brands through word of mouth; converting fans to consumers is a more challenging proposition.

The Power of Complaining

Key Lime Pie, WIN! Hotel Wi-Fi, FAIL

Service recovery is a key initiative that most brand customer service departments are tasked with fulfilling. In the past, consumer complaints occurred out of the public eye; consumers complained directly to the brand via mail, fax, call, e-mail, website form submission, or chat. Another consumer's exposure to consumer complaints was typically limited, coming from traditional word of mouth where consumers shared with their Wi-Fi Internet access about bad experiences. Today, customer complaining is public on social media which reaches a wide audience in most cases.

In the early days of Omni Hotels & Resorts' participation on Twitter, the eCommerce team saw a tweet complaining about Wi-Fi failures at the Jacksonville, Florida (USA) location. This tweet praised the hotel's key lime pie but labeled the Wi-Fi as a failure. The Omni team was monitoring Twitter for feedback on the brand and alerted the local team to the issue. Within minutes, the hotel management had contacted the customer to apologize and the Wi-Fi was restored. What Omni corporate did not know is that the tweeter was actually a speaker at a technology-focused conference at the hotel. By listening to the conversation in social media,

Omni was able to identify a problem, resolve it, and delight the customer. The result was a mention at the conference on the competence that Omni's team showed in social listening, and the conference attendees generated positive word of mouth. In this case, a negative was quickly turned into a positive, resulting in a successful service recovery. Many more cases exist where this outcome is not as positive and a double failure results.

United Breaks Guitars or Band Breaks United's Reputation

In 2008, Dave Carroll flew United Airlines while on tour with his band. From his window seat, he saw his $3,500 guitar handled roughly, which resulted in a total loss of the instrument. When United Airlines refused to resolve the issue after many touch points, Carroll decided to use his musical talent to share his story. Writing the ode "United Breaks Guitars," Carroll shared his tale and released the accompanying music video on YouTube (Figure 6.2). The music video has accumulated over 13 million views as of January 2014.[5] While word of mouth related to this incident is impressive, the possible impact on United's market value is more staggering. According to the *London Times*, the stock price tumbled 10 percent during the time period of the media coverage; this change in value was equivalent to $180 million in market value.[6] Although causation cannot be argued here, at a minimum, additional negative publicity likely exacerbated any other issues during this time.

Figure 6.2 United Breaks Guitars depicts the epic guitar toss

In this case, the company was focused on the timing of Carroll's claim, which occurred outside of the 24-hour window for reporting an incident. This could have been resolved for $3,500 in the form of a reimbursement or replaced instrument. Instead, United encountered a maelstrom of negative publicity. With social media allowing incidents like this to snowball and go viral with the click of a button, firms like United may wish to consider the long-term consequences instead of the immediate policy issues. Exploring the potential fallout of these issues on social media will provide insights when incidents are worth resolving and when standard guideline rules should be disregarded or even changed. As a result of this incident, Carroll released a book, aptly titled *United Breaks Guitars*, which focuses on the power of social media and the consumer's voice.[7] This incident and Carroll's response are now being used by companies across the world in setting policy, training employees, and investigating how to conduct business in the 21st century.

While both the Omni Hotels and United Airlines examples demonstrate social complaining, they depict two very different outcomes. Social complaining (and praise) raises significant marketing operational impacts that must be considered. First, addressing social media requires both financial and personnel resources. Not only must the social team interact with brand fans and create outgoing brand messages, the team must also be empowered to handle complaints and must possess knowledge of how to redirect complaints. Brands may use a separate Twitter account to monitor complaints on the primary brand account, as American Express does with their @AskAmex on Twitter. Secondly, competent handling of social service issues is critical; the brand must understand the factors at play in social media, including word of mouth, online customer recommendations or advocacy, and the megaphone effect of influential consumers. Resolving issues in an open forum can be tricky. Understanding where rules should be compromised is critical, and also recognizing when bending a rule could set a precedent for other customers is of consideration as well. Understanding a customer's value to the firm is also critical, as those with the most influence have the potential to impact the brand more strongly than those who are not taken seriously by their network. As social media channels become integrated more seamlessly into more firm operations, processes for effectively resolving issues will be established. And, if the brand is endeared to consumers, resolving issues will serve to protect the brand.

Deputizing Brand Fans to Support the Brand

How May I Help You?

Many brand supporters may informally monitor information about a brand out of curiosity or in an effort to become expert on the brand. For other experienced customers, the brand may request them to become brand ambassadors to help reduce anxiety for new and potential customers. Online men's clothier, Indochino, asks its past customers to advise prospective consumers on the quality and service provided by the company. Indochino also features photos of consumers wearing its brand on social media channels like Pinterest and Instagram (Figure 6.3). When a Twitter user requests information from others who have purchased an Indochino custom suit, the brand shares the tweet with its own followers to solicit tips and consumer experiences. This encourages prospects to interact with past customers. When purchasing menswear online, particularly a custom suit, seeing actual customers in their clothing helps alleviate worries. Again, the reference group becomes a powerful tool for marketers. When a potential customer of Indochino custom suits sees someone like himself or his body type, he identifies with that community

Figure 6.3 Custom suit firm Indochino's Pinterest Customer Wall of Fame

member and gains confidence in his ability to wear Indochino's clothing. Effectively, the brand uses its customers as models to show what real people look like in the clothing, as opposed to the professional models seen in traditional advertising.

Informal Brand Ambassadors

Brand ambassadors and informal service providers provide companies with de facto employees at no cost. The mobile and desktop note taking application Evernote serves as an example. Passionate users volunteer to be Evernote Ambassadors, segmented by geography, expertise, and language. These passionate users volunteer both time and expertise to support the Evernote brand and resolve user issues (Figure 6.4).

Ambassadors receive no compensation but have strong ties to the Evernote brand and functionality. Through Ambassador biographies and blogs, these passionate users share various ways they use the software, which helps increase service adoption, improve user retention, and encourage premium subscriptions. The users highlight which devices they use with Evernote and how they capture, record, and organize information. See Figure 6.5 for an example of an ambassador blog.

Figure 6.4 The global Evernote ambassador community—Just a click away

I use Evernote, Everywhere

- Mac
- Windows
- iPhone
- Web Clipper
- Evernote Food

I love…

- Call Trunk for recording phone interviews

Evernote: My Food Writing Companion

Figure 6.5 Evernote blog from Evernote Ambassador[8]

Consumers have high service expectations and some brands may not have the resources to support a large service team. Limited resources make it impossible to react at the speed required for social media. Having a volunteer army of brand fans may be an effective strategy; however, several factors must be taken into consideration. First, ambassadors must have involvement at a high level to warrant a personal commitment. Second, ambassador recognition and status are important for fostering an engaged and responsive ambassador network. Thus, highly knowledgeable and respected opinion leaders are necessary. Third, to appear robust, there must be sufficient content generated and a high level of responsiveness. The perception of a lackluster effort can lead online consumers to infer that the brand does not warrant support. Fourth, some effort must be made to manage the ambassadors, as it can be difficult to monitor the accuracy of information shared, influence the tone of communication, and ensure that the process does not evolve into something completely out of the control of the firm. This requires minimal resources, but a well-thought-out strategy and continual monitoring.

Key Takeaways

- Joining a brand's Facebook page has no barriers to entry; anyone can join the page. Joining is not indicative of whether the "fan" will convert to consumer.
- Brands like Virgin Galactic should invest in social media. Fans of the parent brand will aspire to the new brands, despite price barriers that prevent most consumers from ever experiencing the product.
- Social media servicing is no longer an option; it is a mandatory.
- What could be a relatively minor, isolated incident can spread virally through video and visual media, such as YouTube and Instagram. Social listening allows the brand to monitor and respond to issues.
- An effective response, such as Omni Hotels' response to a Wi-Fi outage, can result in legendary customer service word of mouth, as evidenced by the technology conference tweets.
- An issue, such as United Breaks Guitars, is no longer a consumer-to-brand private interaction. Every customer service interaction has the potential to be a public event. Brands must decide what leeway they have in customer resolution (and what resolution might set a dangerous precedent).
- Brands have the opportunity to leverage brand community members to reassure potential customers, such as Indochino's feedback requests via Twitter.
- Leveraging actual customer photos enact the power of the reference group, particularly where there may be potential objections that prevent purchasing online. Seeing actual users helps prospects identify with someone "like himself or herself."
- An Ambassador program shows use cases for a product via blogs, providing content in social media. The brand must have a strategy to make this content robust and valuable or risk negative consequences.

CHAPTER 7

Past, Present, and Future of Digital Brand Communities

You have to think of your brand as a kind of myth. A myth is a compelling story that is archetypal.... It has to have emotional content and all of the themes of a great story: mystery, magic, adventure, intrigue, conflicts, contradiction, paradox.

—Deepak Chopra[1]

We have discussed how brands are using digital marketing tools to build brand community. These online communities are widely accepted and used by consumers, and brands are engaging across these media. While the community format is preexisting on the social media sites, the competent marketer invests resources in engaging consumers, creating a two-way dialogue, and fostering positive brand sentiment. It is not enough to simply post content; the community requires participation. Successful marketers understand the importance of relational characteristics in building and fostering an engaged brand community. Positive outcomes of fostering this brand community are myriad, including gauging consumer sentiment, resolving potential customer issues, and advancing new and existing relationships.

Brands are fortunate that social media sites exist for engaging consumers in brand community; originally that was not the case. Prior to the development of digital communities and message boards (and later social media), brand fans organized and shared their brand experiences in person through events, rallies, social gatherings, and other communal activities. Brands participated by organizing some events, so the firm required more organization. Today, events still occur, but online communities supplement these gatherings. Content from these events is shared to social media, and brands and consumers both create content and excitement for the brand online.

Each of the proceeding chapters discussed the various factors contributing to building, maintaining, and benefiting from brand communities using digital and social media. Chapter 1 introduced the concepts of brand, relational, and community characteristics, each of which is an important qualification for online brand communities. These were laid out in Figure 1.1 and are repeated here in Figure 7.1.

Ongoing relationships with customers can lead to brand loyalty and create value.[2] Brand managers build successful online brand communities when they promote specific brand characteristics, relational characteristics, and community characteristics. The necessary first precursor is a strong brand—be competent, have a strong reputation, and be perceived as representing quality. These brand characteristics lead to brand identification and identity salience related to the brand for the consumer. The more consumers identify with the brand, enjoy their brand experiences, and are engaged in social media, the stronger the tie with the brand becomes. Managers can work to influence the importance of both the reference group and the marketing messages to the consumers. The relevance of the reference group and the relevance of the message will influence identification with owners and identity importance, which in turn build brand community. When individuals identify with others in the group and the salience of the brand identity is bolstered, the community and the brand become more important.

In order for consumers to want to interact with the brand via online communities, companies must cultivate a strong brand first. The efforts and concerns that brand managers should consider for communicating

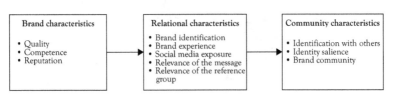

Figure 7.1 Brand, relational, and community characteristics leading to brand community

brand quality, competence, and reputation online were discussed in Chapter 2. Providing consumers with a strong brand increases the probability of earning brand loyalty and the promise of long-term profitable relationships with these consumers.[3] Core relational factors can be used to enhance relationship building as a necessary precursor to developing a deeper brand relationship with consumers. Impact of relational factors such as brand identification, brand experience, social media exposure, message relevance, and reference group was discussed in Chapter 3. Chapter 4 focused on community factors such as identification with others and identity salience for building brand community. Chapter 5 explored differences between and integration of traditional face-to-face brand communities versus online brand communities. The importance of brand fans and brand ambassadors, and the roles consumers play online to support the brand were discussed in Chapter 6. Throughout all of these chapters, anecdotes were given that serve as excellent examples of where brands benefited or paid a price as a consequence of online brand management.

Social media is a powerful tool in the Integrated Marketing Communications mix that firms can cultivate. By managing the social media platform, companies can engage consumers through online relationships. This online consumer engagement then extends to engagement with other consumers loyal to the brand, leading to identity salience and brand loyalty. Companies can build loyal customers with brand communities. This relationship with loyal customers creates value for the firm. Collaboration with consumers in online brand communities teaches marketers how consumers use the products and what role the brand plays in the life of the consumer. Marketers have the ability to cocreate messages and product customizations with key consumers. Managers are encouraged to foster brand and social network use in online brand communities. In organic communities, managers should encourage customers to build these practices. Marketing managers need to promote engagement in online brand communities by providing opportunities for consumers to interact and create content on their own. Focusing on the practices of consumers with salient identities can foster opinion leadership. Furthermore, firms can rely on the brand community to engage in product development and brand extension.

In the future, technology will allow more collaboration between brand community participants and the brands they support. From collaborative product development through participant-generated ideas to on-demand 3D printing of limited edition consumer-designed product variations, opportunities for deeper community to brand engagement will be amplified by new technology. As consumers cocreate their brand experiences, they will continue to share their product consumption experience through social media to their personal networks. As their friends and fellow brand community participants provide feedback and validation across social media sharing and within the communities, relevant and important identities related to the brand are reinforced. Evolving technology will play a greater role. These shared and consumer cocreated experiences will deepen the relationship with the brand. The brand, in turn, will use the time-tested community and relationship-centric approach in fostering community. Technology may advance, but fostering and cultivating relationships remains key.

Key Takeaways

- Brand community has been around for decades, but it will evolve with technology in how it is facilitated and how the consumer cocreates brand experiences.
- Brands should invest in social media as a way to build relationships with consumers and form a brand community; regardless of the medium, relationships are the key.
- Brand experiences can be relived through social media (and experienced for the first time by a participant's network through shared content).
- Companies should use online brand communities to launch brand experiences; this can then be leveraged with word-of-mouth and social media interactions.
- A key concern for firms is to ensure the relevance of the message and the reference group is appropriate for their brand community.

- Brands have the opportunity to leverage brand community members to develop salient identities; these consumers will be brand champions.
- Leveraging customer identity salience is a powerful way to cultivate brand equity.
- Technology will advance, and consumers will be able create new products and variations with brands. This cocreation will be shared through social media channels.
- Regardless of technology advancements, the brand must invest in fostering community and engaging supporters of the brand.

Notes

Chapter 1

1. McAlexander, Schouten, and Koenig (2002, 38).
2. Fournier (1998).
3. Muñiz and O'Guinn (2001).
4. Wang, Butt, and Wei (2011).
5. Wang, Butt, and Wei (2011).
6. Adjei, Noble, and Noble (2009).
7. Wang, Butt, and Wei (2011).
8. McAlexander, Schouten, and Koenig (2002).
9. Wilcox and Stephen (2013).
10. Szmigin and Reppel (2004).
11. Kozinets et al. (2010).
12. Daboll (2011).
13. McQuarrie, Miller, and Phillips (2013).
14. Wortham, Goel, and Perlroth (2013).
15. Wilcox and Stephen (2013).
16. Schouten, McAlexander, and Koenig (2007).
17. Bennett (2013).
18. Stadd (2013).
19. Berger and Iyengar (2013).
20. McAlexander, Schouten, and Koenig (2002).
21. Dholakia and Herrmann (2005).

Chapter 2

1. Facebook (2013).
2. Parasurman et al. (1998).
3. Zeithaml, Berry, and Parasuraman (1996).
4. Volvo Cars U.S. (2013).
5. Virgin America (2014).
6. Hunt (2000).

7. Hunt (2000).

8. Ashforth and Mael (1989).

9. Dutton, Dukerich, and Harquail (1994).

10. Bruwer and Alant (2009).

11. "Twitter/navaja1cortes: Thank You @AskAmex and …" (2013).

12. Freed (2013).

13. Walsh and Beatty (2007).

14. Muñiz and O'Guinn (2001).

15. Ganesan (1994).

16. https://twitter.com/dkny/status/335025654141681665

17. "Sheraton Gunter San Antonio Guest Reviews" (2003).

18. Morgan and Hunt (1994).

19. Cone (2008).

Chapter 3

1. Davidson, McNeill, and Ferguson (2007).

2. Laverie, Kleine, and Kleine (2002); Davidson, McNeill, and Ferguson (2007).

3. Fournier (1998).

4. Samsung Mobile USA (2013).

5. Coca-Cola (2013).

6. Coca-Cola (2013).

7. Koh (2015).

8. Schneider and Rodgers (1993); Feick and Price (1987).

9. Avis Car Rental (2013).

10. Wortham (2013).

11. Burt (2013).

12. Shareen (2013).

13. Honan (2013).

14. Systrom (2013).

15. Snapchat (2015).

16. Sheth and Sisodia (1999).

17. Humphrey and Laverie (2011).

18. Netflix (2013).

19. MailChimp (2013).

20. Ferraro, Bettman, and Chartrand (2009).

21. Ferraro, Bettman, and Chartrand (2009).

22. Foursquare.com (2015).

23. Naylor, Lamberton, and West (2012).

24. Humphrey (2013).

25. Neiman Marcus (2013).

26. Neiman Marcus (2015a).

27. Neiman Marcus (2015b).

28. Marcus (2013).

Chapter 4

1. Bhattacharya, Rao, and Glynn (1995).

2. Aaker (1997).

3. Underwood, Bond, and Baer (2001).

4. Madupu and Krishnan (2008).

5. Davidson, McNeill, and Ferguson (2007).

6. McAlexander, Schouten, and Koenig (2002).

7. Cova and Pace (2006).

8. Rosso and Fabio (2014).

9. Vespa Americas (2014).

10. Callero and Piliavin (1983); Stryker and Serpe (1994).

11. McAlexander, Schouten, and Koenig (2002).

12. Wang, Butt, and Wei (2011).

13. Bilton (2014).

14. Rachau (2014).

15. Laverie et al. (2002).

16. McAlexander, Schouten, and Koenig (2002, p. 42).

17. Quatami (2014).

Chapter 5

1. Chang (2012).

2. DKNY (2011).

3. Yi (2015).

4. Lockwood (2015).

5. Facebook (2014).

6. Chen (2013).

7. Elmer-DeWitt (2015).

8. Apple Inc. (2015).

9. Molen (2013).

10. Reitsma (2013).

11. PBS (2014b).

12. "Twitter/Tomandlorenzo: Time to Get Your #DowntonPBS …" (2014).

13. PBS (2014a).

14. "Lady Mary's Eyebrows (L_MarysEyebrows) on Twitter" (2014).

15. www.socialguide.com/nielsen-twitter-tv-ratings/

16. http://www.socialguide.com/nielsen-launches-nielsen-twitter-tv-ratings/

17. Nielsen Social (2013).

18. "Trending Shows - Tvtag" (2014).

19. "Trending Shows - Tvtag" (2014).

Chapter 6

1. Oliver (1999).

2. Muñiz and O'Guinn (2001).

3. Chaudhuri and Holbrook (2001).

4. Virgin (2014).

5. Sonsofmaxwell (2009).

6. Ayres (2009).

7. Carroll (2014).

8. Hickey (2012).

Chapter 7

1. Schurenberg (2011).

2. McAlexander, Schouten, and Koenig (2002).

3. Bhattacharya, Rao, and Glynn (1995).

Bibliography

Aaker, J.L. 1997. "Dimensions of Brand Personality." *Journal of Marketing Research* 34, no. 3, pp. 347–56. doi:10.2307/3151897

Adjei, M.T., S.M. Noble, and C.H. Noble. November 13, 2009. "The Influence of C2C Communications in Online Brand Communities on Customer Purchase Behavior." *Journal of the Academy of Marketing Science* 38, no. 5, pp. 634–53. doi:10.1007/s11747-009-0178-5

Ang, L. October 3, 2011. "Is SCRM Really a Good Social Media Strategy?" *Journal of Database Marketing and Customer Strategy Management* 18, no. 3, pp. 149–53. doi:10.1057/dbm.2011.22

Apple Inc. 2015. *Apple Spring Forward Event.* USA: Apple, Inc. www.apple.com/ live/2015-mar-event/

Ashforth, B.E., and F. Mael. 1989. "Social Identity Theory and the Organization." *Academy of Management Review* 14, no. 1, pp. 20–39. http://amr.aom.org/ content/14/1/20.short

Ayres, C. 2009. "Revenge Is Best Served Cold—on YouTube." *The Times.* www. thetimes.co.uk/tto/law/columnists/article2051377.ece

Avis Car Rental. 2013. "@Avis." Twitter.com. N.p. [Web].

Bennett, S. 2013. "Twitter Users—AllTwitter." MediaBistro. www.mediabistro. com/alltwitter/tag/twitter-users

Berger, J., and R. Iyengar. October 2013. "Communication Channels and Word of Mouth: How the Medium Shapes the Message." *Journal of Consumer Research* 40, no. 3, pp. 567–79. doi:10.1086/671345

Bhattacharya, C.B., H. Rao, and M.A. Glynn. 1995. "Understanding the Bond of Identification: An Investigation of Its Correiates Among Art Museum Members." *Journal of Marketing* 59, pp. 46–57. doi:10.2307/1252327

Bilton, N. 2014. "On Big Stage of CES, Innovation Is in Background." *New York Times,* January 13. http://bits.blogs.nytimes.com/2014/01/12/disruptions-at-ces-a-big-stage-for-big-dreams-but-fewer-surprises/?_php=true&_ type=blogs&_r=0

Bruwer, J., and K. Alant. 2009. "The Hedonic Nature of Wine Tourism Consumption: An Experiential View." *International Journal of Wine Business* 21, no. 3, pp. 235–57. doi:10.1108/17511060910985962

Burt, J. 2013. "Jordan Burt's Post on Vine." Vine.com. N.p. [Web].

Callero, P.L., and J.A. Piliavin. 1983. "Developing a Commitment to Blood Donation: The Impact of One's First Experience." *Journal of Applied Social Psychology* 13, no. 1, pp. 1–16. doi:10.1111/j.1559-1816.1983.tb00883.x

Carroll, D. 2014. "Dave's Book!" Dave Carroll Music. www.davecarrollmusic. com/book/

Chang, B.-S. 2012, February 12. "P.R. Girl Revealed as P.R. Executive." *New York Times*, p. E9. Retrieved from http://www.nytimes.com/2012/02/16/fashion/ aliza-licht-unnamed-twitter-fashion-star-comes-out-on-youtube.html?_r=0

Chaudhuri, A., and M.B. Holbrook. 2001. "The Chain of Effects from Brand Trust and Brand Affect to Brand Performance: The Role of Brand Loyalty." *Journal of Marketing* 65, no. 2, pp. 81–93. doi:10.1509/jmkg.65.2.81. 18255

Chen, B.X. 2013. "Apple Enters Net Radio's Busy Field." *New York Times*, June 10. www.nytimes.com/2013/06/10/technology/apple-enters-busy-field-of- streaming-radio.html?pagewanted=all

Coca-Cola. 2013. "@CocaCola." Twitter.com. https://twitter.com/CocaCola/ status/413008340835258368

Coca-Cola. 2013. "@CocaCola." Twitter.com. N.p. [Web].

Cone. 2008. "2008 Business in Social Media Study." Boston, MA. www. conecomm.com/2008-business-in-social-media-study

Cova, B., and S. Pace. 2006. "Brand Community of Convenience Products: New Forms of Customer Empowerment—the Case 'my Nutella The Community.'" *European Journal of Marketing* 40, no. 9/10, pp. 1087–105. doi:10.1108/03090560610681023

Daboll, P. 2011. "Celebriities in Advertising Are Almost Big Waste of Money." *Ad Age*, January. http://adage.com/article/cmo-strategy/celebrities-ads-lead- greater-sales/148174/

Davidson, L., L. McNeill, and S. Ferguson. 2007. "Magazine Communities: Brand Community Formation in Magazine Consumption." *International Journal of Sociology and Social Policy* 27, no. 5/6, pp. 208–20. doi:10.1108/01443330710757249

DKNY. 2012. "DKNY #UK2012." YouTube.

DKNY. 2011. "The Real DKNY PR Girl." YouTube. www.youtube.com/ watch?v=p3ImtnUtueU

Dutton, J.E., J.M. Dukerich, and C.V. Harquail. 1994. "Organizational Images and Member Identification." *Administrative Science Quarterly* 39, no. 2, pp. 239–63. www.jstor.org/stable/10.2307/2393235

Elmer-DeWitt, P. 2015. "Apple Watch Rumor Round-Up." *Fortune*. http:// fortune.com/2015/03/07/apple-watch-rumor-round-up/

Facebook. 2013. "How to Use Facebook for Business Marketing." Facebook. com. www.facebook.com/business/overview

Feick, L.F., and L.L. Price. 1987. "The Market Maven: A Diffuser of Marketplace Information." *Journal of Marketing* 51, no. 1, pp. 83–97. doi:10.2307/1251146

Ferraro, R., J.R. Bettman, and T.L. Chartrand. February 2009. "The Power of Strangers: The Effect of Incidental Consumer Brand Encounters on Brand Choice." *Journal of Consumer Research* 35, no. 5, pp. 729–41. doi:10.1086/592944

Fisher, T. 2009. "ROI in Social Media: A Look at the Arguments." *Journal of Database Marketing and Customer Strategy Management* 16, no. 3, pp. 189–95. doi:10.1057/dbm.2009.16

Fournier, S. March 1998. "Consumers and Their Brands: Developing Relationship Theory in Consumer Research." *Journal of Consumer Research* 24, no. 4, pp. 343–73. www.jstor.org/stable/10.1086/209515

Foursquare.com. 2015. "Taco Diner—Uptown." Foursquare.com. N.p. [Web].

Freed, V. 2013. "Vicki Freed." Facebook.com. www.facebook.com/photo.php?fbid=514833381907423&set=a.417519571638805.93227.415067658550663&type=1

Ganesan, S. 2011. "Determinants of Long-Term in Buyer-Seller Orientation Relationships." *Journal of Marketing* 58, no. 2, pp. 1–19.

Ganesan, S. 1994. "Determinants of Long-Term Orientation in Buyer-Seller Relationships." *Journal of Marketing* 58, no. 2. p. 1. doi:10.2307/1252265

Hickey, K.F. 2012. "Evernote and Evernote Food: A Food Writer's Companions." *Evernote Blog.* http://blog.evernote.com/blog/2012/03/05/evernote-and-evernote-food-a-food-writers-companions/

Honan, M. 2013. "How Vine Climbed to the Top of the Social Media Ladder." *Wired.* www.wired.com/2013/06/qq_vine/

Humphrey, W.F., Jr. 2013. "Neiman Marcus: Making Fashion Social Through Strategy and Execution." *Huffington Post.* www.huffingtonpost.com/lin-humphrey/neiman-marcus-making-fashion_b_2679007.html

Humphrey, W.F., and D.A Laverie. 2011. "Driving Frequency with Mobile Social Networks (MSN) and the Mediating Effects of Price and Quota Promotions." *International Journal of Mobile Marketing* 6, no. 2, pp. 46–59.

Koh, Y. 2015. "Pinterest to Soon Add a 'Buy' Button." *Wall Street Journal,* June 2. www.wsj.com/articles/pinterest-to-soon-add-a-buy-button-news-digest-1433289211

Kozinets, R.V. 2002. "The Field Behind the Screen: Using Netnography for Marketing Research in Online Communities." *Journal of Marketing Research* 39, pp. 61–72. doi:10.1509/jmkr.39.1.61.18935

"Lady Mary's Eyebrows (L_MarysEyebrows) on Twitter." 2014. Twitter.com. https://twitter.com/L_MarysEyebrows

Laverie, D.A., R.E. Kleine, and S.S. Kleine. March 2002. "Reexamination and Extension of Kleine, Kleine, and Kernan's Social Identity Model of Mundane Consumption: The Mediating Role of Appraisal Process." *Journal of Consumer Research* 28, pp. 659–69.

Licht, A. 2015. *Leave Your Mark: Land Your Dream Job. Kill It in Your Career. Rock Social Media.* 1st ed. New York City, NY: Grand Central Publishing.

Lockwood, L. 2015. "Aliza Licht to Exit Donna Karan International in the Fall." WWD. Retrieved October 10, 2015, from http://wwd.com/media-news/marketing/aliza-licht-dkny-pr-girl-to-exit-in-the-fall-10201661/

Madupu, V., and B. Krishnan. 2008. "The Relationship Between Online Brand Community Participation and Consciousness of Kind, Moral Responsibility, and Shared Rituals and Traditions." *Advances in Consumer Research* 35, no. 3, pp. 853–54. http://search.ebscohost.com/login.aspx?direct=true&db=bth&AN=35063950&site=ehost-live

MailChimp. 2013. "@MailChimp." Twitter.com. https://twitter.com/MailChimp/status/411261014458785792

Marcus, N. 2013. "Neiman Marcus on Instagram: 'Around the Store: Diana Vreeland Holiday Window at NM Beverly Hills. #OnlyatNM.'" Instagram.com. N.p. [Web].

McAlexander, J.H., J.W. Schouten, and H.F. Koenig. January 2002. "Building Brand Community." *Journal of Marketing* 66, no. 1, pp. 38–55. www.jstor.org/stable/10.2307/3203368

McQuarrie, E.F., J. Miller, and B.J. Phillips. June 2013. "The Megaphone Effect: Taste and Audience in Fashion Blogging." *Journal of Consumer Research* 40, no. 1, pp. 136–58. doi:10.1086/669042

Molen, B. 2013. "Apple's Next-Generation iPhone Liveblog!" Engadget.com. www.engadget.com/2013/09/10/apple-iphone-liveblog-2013/

Morgan, R.M., and S.D. Hunt. July 1994. "The Commitment-Trust Theory of Relationship Marketing." *Journal of Marketing* 58, no. 3, pp. 20–38. doi:10.2307/1252308

Muñiz, A.M., Jr., and T.C. O'Guinn. March 2001. "Brand Community." *Journal of Consumer Research* 27, no. 4, pp. 412–32. www.jstor.org/stable/10.1086/319618

Naylor, R., C. Lamberton, and P.M. West. November 2012. "Beyond the 'Like' Button: The Impact of Mere Virtual Presence on Brand Evaluations and Purchase Intentions in Social Media Settings." *Journal of Marketing* 76, no. 6, pp. 105–20. http://papers.ssrn.com/sol3/papers.cfm?abstract_id=2078586

Neiman Marcus. 2013. "Neiman Marcus." Instagram.com. http://instagram.com/p/iH2ou3rT4S/

Netflix. 2013. "Netflix Banner Ad." Facebook.com. http://movies.netflix.com/WiMovie/Lilyhammer/70221438?mqso=81278483&noredir=true

Nielsen Social. 2013. "Nielsen Launches 'Nielsen Twitter TV Ratings.'" Social TV Insights—Social Guide. www.socialguide.com/nielsen-launches-nielsen-twitter-tv-ratings/

Nielsen Social. 2013. "The Follow-Back: Understanding the Two-Way Causal Influence Between Twitter Activity and TV Viewership." Nielsen.com. www. nielsen.com/us/en/newswire/2013/the-follow-back--understanding-the-two-way-causal-influence-betw.html

Neiman Marcus. 2013. "Neiman Marcus (@neimanmarcus) Instagram photos and video." Instagram.com. N.p. [Web].

Neiman Marcus. 2015a. "Neiman Marcus (@neimanmarcus)|Twitter." Twitter. com. N.p. [Web].

Neiman Marcus. 2015b. "Neiman Marcus on Pinterest." Pinterest.com. N.p. [Web].

Oliver, R.L. 1999. "Whence Consumer Loyalty?" *Journal of Marketing* 63, p. 33. doi:10.2307/1252099

Pathak, S. 2013. "These Vine Celebs Made $10,000 in Six Seconds on Their Mobile Phones." *Advertising Age.* http://adage.com/article/digital/vine-users-team-brands-talent-agency/243773/

PBS. 2014a. "Twitter/PBS: Proper Twitter Attire ---> ..." Twitter.com. https:// twitter.com/PBS/status/288146275248009216

PBS. 2014b. "Two-Hour Premiere of 'Downton Abbey, Season 4' on MASTERPIECE Highest Rated Drama Premiere in PBS History." PBS.org. www.pbs.org/about/news/archive/2014/downton-abbey-4-premiere/

Quatami, A. 2014. "Andy Qutami—Photos of Pebble." Facebook.com. www.facebook.com/photo.php?fbid=724447614235013&set=o.4108 52228944681&type=1

Rachau, A. 2014. "Twitter/Amandarachau: @JohnLegere Breaking up Never ..." Twitter.com. https://twitter.com/amandarachau/status/423539413226 770432

Reitsma, R. 2013. "The Data Digest: Listening Data Reveals Fluctuating Consumer Sentiment Around Apple's 5s and 5c Iphone Launch." Forrester Research. http://blogs.forrester.com/reineke_reitsma/13-10-11-the_data_digest_listening_data_reveals_fluctuating_consumer_sentiment_around_apples_5s_and_5c_ipho

René, A., D. Utpal, and A. Herrmann. July 2005. "The Social Influence of Brand Community: Evidence from European Car Clubs." *Journal of Marketing* 69, no. 3, pp. 19–34.

Rosso, S., and M. Fabio. 2014. "World Nutella Day." Facebook.com.

"Samsung Mobile USA." 2013. Facebook.com. www.facebook.com/photo.php? fbid=10151699228691786&set=a.59297021785.81337.7224956785&type=1

Schneider, K.C., and W.C. Rodgers. 1993. "Generalized Marketplace Influencers' (Market Mavens') Attitudes Toward Direct Mail as a Source of Information." *Journal of Direct Marketing* 7, no. 4, pp. 20–28. doi:10.1002/dir.4000070405

Schomer, S. 2010. "Neiman Marcus' CEO Karen Katz to Sell Luxury Through Social Media."

Schouten, J.W., J.H. McAlexander, and H.F. Koenig. May 9, 2007. "Transcendent Customer Experience and Brand Community." *Journal of the Academy of Marketing Science* 35, no. 3, pp. 357–68. doi:10.1007/s11747-007-0034-4

Schurenberg, E. 2011. "Deepak Chopra: The Two Questions Every Business Leader Has to Ask." CBS MoneyWatch. www.cbsnews.com/news/deepak-chopra-the-two-questions-every-business-leader-has-to-ask/

"Sheraton Gunter San Antonio Guest Reviews." 2013. Starwood Hotels. www.starwoodhotels.com/sheraton/property/reviews/index.html?propertyID=1291

Sheth, J.N., and R.S. Sisodia. January 1, 1999. "Revisiting Marketing's Lawlike Generalizations." *Journal of the Academy of Marketing Science* 27, no. 1, pp. 71–87. doi:10.1177/0092070399271006

Simmons, R.G., J.A. Piliavin, and P.L. Callero. 1992. "Giving Blood: The Development of an Altruistic Identity." *Contemporary Sociology*. doi:10.2307/2075899

Snapchat. 2015. "Ads Snapchat." Retrieved from www.snapchat.com/ads

Sonsofmaxwell. 2009. "United Breaks Guitars." YouTube. www.youtube.com/watch?v=5YGc4zOqozo

Stadd, A. 2013. "Facebook and Pinterest Dwarf Twitter in Referral Traffic [CHART]—AllTwitter." MediaBistro. www.mediabistro.com/alltwitter/facebook-pinterest-dwarf-twitter-referral-traffic_b50548

Stryker, S., and R.T. Serpe. 1994. "Identity Salience and Psychological Centrality: Equivalent, Overlapping, or Complementary Concepts?" *Social Psychology Quarterly* 57, no. 1, p. 16. http://doi.org/10.2307/2786972

Systrom, K. 2013. "Introducing Video on Instagram." Instagram.com. N.p. [Web].

Szmigin, I., L. Canning, and A.E. Reppel. 2005. "Online Community: Enhancing the Relationship Marketing Concept Through Customer Bonding." *International Journal of Service Industry Management* 16, no. 5, pp. 480–96. www.emeraldinsight.com/journals.htm?articleid=1523883&show=abstract

Taco D. 2013. "Taco Diner." Foursquare.com.

"Trending Shows—Tvtag." 2014. Tvtag.com. http://tvtag.com/guide/tv_shows/trending

"Twitter/Navaja1cortes: Thank You @AskAmex and …." 2013. Twitter. https://twitter.com/navaja1cortes/status/395552260048310272

"Twitter/Tomandlorenzo: Time to Get Your #DowntonPBS …." 2014. Twitter.com. https://twitter.com/tomandlorenzo/status/430159063054168065

Underwood, R., E. Bond, and R. Baer. 2001. "Building Service Brands via Social Identity: Lessons from the Sports Marketplace." *Journal of Marketing Theory and Practice* 9, no. 1, pp. 1–13. www.jstor.org/stable/10.2307/40470193

Vespa Americas. 2014. "(2) Vespa Americas—8 Vespas, 4000 Miles and 3 Weeks of Adventure …." Facebook.com. www.facebook.com/vespausa/posts/10152557157498327

Virgin. 2014. "Find a Virgin Company." Tvtag.com. www.virgin.com/company

Virgin America. 2014. "Favorites." Twitter. https://twitter.com/VirginAmerica/favorites

Volvo Cars US. 2013. "Volvo Cars US." Facebook.com. www.facebook.com/photo.php?fbid=10152041485054489&set=a.396307149488.160397.339744344488&type=1

Walsh, G., and S.E. Beatty. 2007. "Customer-Based Corporate Reputation of a Service Firm: Scale Development and Validation." *Journal of the Academy of Marketing Science* 35, pp. 127–43. doi:10.1007/s11747-007-0015-7

Wang, Y.J., O.J. Butt, and J. Wei. 2011. "My Identity Is My Membership: A Longitudinal Explanation of Online Brand Community Members' Behavioral Characteristics." *Journal of Brand Management* 19, no. 1, pp. 45–56. doi:10.1057/bm.2011.28

Wilcox, K., and A.T. Stephen. June 2013. "Are Close Friends the Enemy? Online Social Networks, Self-Esteem, and Self-Control." *Journal of Consumer Research* 40, no. 1, pp. 90–103. doi:10.1086/668794

Woodcock, N., A. Green, and M. Starkey. March 2011. "Social CRM as a Business Strategy." *Journal of Database Marketing and Customer Strategy Management* 18, no. 1 pp. 50–64. doi:10.1057/dbm.2011.7

Wortham, J. 2013. "Vine, Twitter's New Video Tool, Hits 13 Million Users." *New York Times.* http://bits.blogs.nytimes.com/2013/06/03/vine-twitters-new-video-tool-hits-13-million-users/?_r=0

Wortham, J., V. Goel, and N. Perlroth. 2013. "Facebook, Still Dominant, Strives to Keep Cachet." *New York Times*, November 18. www.nytimes.com/2013/11/18/technology/facebook-strives-to-keep-its-cachet.html?pagewanted=all

Yi, D. 2015. "Farewell, DKNY PR Girl: The Fashion Brand Breaks with Its Sassy Mascot." Retrieved October 10, 2015, from http://mashable.com/2015/08/11/goodbye-dkny-pr-girl/#983jaqB6Hgqx

Zeithaml, V.A., L.L. Berry, and A. Parasuraman. 1996. "The Behavioral Consequences of Service Quality." *Journal of Marketing* 60, no. 2, pp. 31–46. www.jstor.org/stable/10.2307/1251929

Index

OTHER TITLES IN DIGITAL AND SOCIAL MEDIA MARKETING AND ADVERTISING COLLECTION
Victoria L. Crittenden, Babson College, Editor

- *Viral Marketing and Social Networks* by Maria Petrescu
- *Herding Cats: A Strategic Approach to Social Media Marketing* by Andrew Rohm and Michael Weiss
- *Social Roots: Why Social Innovations Are Creating the Influence Economy* by Cindy Gordon, John P. Girard, and Andrew Weir
- *Social Media Branding For Small Business: The 5-Sources Model* by Robert Davis
- *A Beginner's Guide to Mobile Marketing* by Karen Mishra and Molly Garris
- *Social Content Marketing for Entrepreneurs* by James M. Barry
- *Digital Privacy in the Marketplace: Perspectives on the Information Exchange* by George Milne
- *This Note's For You: Popular Music + Advertising = Marketing Excellence* by David Allan
- *Digital Marketing Management: A Handbook for the Current (or Future) CEO* by Debra Zahay
- *Corporate Branding in Facebook Fan Pages: Ideas for Improving Your Brand Value* by Eliane Pereira Zamith Brito, Maria Carolina Zanette, Benjamin Rosenthal, Carla Caires Abdalla, and Mateus Ferreira
- *Presentation Skills: Educate, Inspire and Engage Your Audience* by Michael Weiss
- *The Connected Consumer* by Dinesh Kumar
- *Mobile Commerce: How It Contrasts, Challenges and Enhances Electronic Commerce* by Esther Swilley

Announcing the Business Expert Press Digital Library

Concise e-books business students need for classroom and research

This book can also be purchased in an e-book collection by your library as

- a one-time purchase,
- that is owned forever,
- allows for simultaneous readers,
- has no restrictions on printing, and
- can be downloaded as PDFs from within the library community.

Our digital library collections are a great solution to beat the rising cost of textbooks. E-books can be loaded into their course management systems or onto students' e-book readers.
The **Business Expert Press** digital libraries are very affordable, with no obligation to buy in future years. For more information, please visit **www.businessexpertpress.com/librarians**. To set up a trial in the United States, please email **sales@businessexpertpress.com**.